Creating Dental Office Systems

Written by:

Denise Ciardello
Janice Janssen
Christopher Ciardello

(OMG! Office Management Guide)
REVISED Copyright © 2015
First Edition, 2010

Denise Ciardello, Janice Janssen and Christopher Ciardello
www.GTSgurus.com

All rights reserved. No part of this book may be reproduced or transmitted in any form or by any means without written permission from the author.

ISBN **978-0-9849977-1-8**

Printed in USA by 48HrBooks (www.48HrBooks.com)

Dedication

We dedicate this book to our loving husbands, Mike and Brad. Without their constant support, encouragement and love, this would have never been possible. And to our children, Chris, Keff, Robbie, Kevin, Nick and Katie; as we strive to be the mothers to guide your way, you continue to teach us what is really important in life. Thank you for understanding, patience and allowing us to dream.

There have been many friends, family and colleagues that have supported us through this process. We are forever grateful to all of you for your honesty, confidence and belief in our ability to tackle, and complete, this project. Judy Logins, you will never know the can of worms that you opened --- **THANK YOU!!**

"Be who you are, and say what you feel;
Because those who mind don't matter,
And those who matter don't mind."

Dr. Seuss

Table of Contents

Dedication 3
Introduction 6
Chapter 1 --**The Purpose of an Office Manager** 9
Chapter 2 – **Productive Scheduling** 49
Chapter 3 – **Optimizing Insurance Systems** 69
Chapter 4 – **Basics of Medical Cross Coding** 107
Chapter 5 – **Handling Hygiene** 131
Chapter 6 – **Treatment Planning** 159
Chapter 7 – **$$ All About the Money $$** 171
Chapter 8 --**The Human Side of Business** 207
Chapter 9 –**Team Meetings** 219
Chapter 10 –**Conflict Resolution** 247
Chapter 11-- **Technology** 259
Glossary 279
About the Authors 293

Introduction

Dental offices are unique in many ways to the typical business. More often than not, there are less than 20 employees, with the majority having less than 10. This prompts the need for cross-training in all areas to fill vacancies due to vacations, illnesses or even bathroom breaks, putting the responsibility squarely on the office manager's shoulders to ensure a smooth transition whether it is for days, weeks or just minutes by maintaining the fundamental systems. More than ever before, it is important to be on top of your game. This is true for business and individuals.

OMG! is designed to assist the brand new office manager realize the necessity to create efficient system; as well as aid the seasoned office manager to recognize any deficiencies in effective protocols in order to successfully manage a dental office.

Our years in dental offices, as team members, software trainers and now as consultants allow us the opportunity to see and understand the challenges the office manager faces. We see the disconnect between knowing what needs to be done and ultimately getting the fundamental systems in place. Our focus as consultants is to create efficient systems and protocols that are second nature so that there is never this division.

This book is not intended to be an end-all, be-all but merely to help the office manager to get on track or stay on track, faster and with relative ease. When working in the trenches all day, it is often easy to lose sight of everything that is required to maintain an efficient, productive business.

> **"Be the change you want to see in the world."**
>
> **Gandhi**

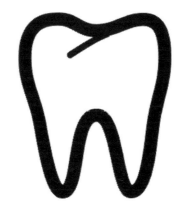

Chapter One

THE PURPOSE
OF AN OFFICE MANAGER

The job of a dental Office Manager is similar to that of a traffic cop at a major intersection in New York City. To maintain control over multiple things while keeping everything flowing, and hopefully making it look effortless.

Henri Fayol was the first person to identify elements or functions of management in his classic 1916 book *Administration Industrielle et Generale.* Oddly enough, the same functions that he identified in his book are still relevant to today's manager. These five basic functions include:

1. **Planning** – Every office has, or should have, goals. There are goals for production, new patients, marketing, purchasing, etc., to name the most common. Some offices have individual procedure goals – X number of crowns, Scaling and Root Planing (SRP) or new ortho cases. Determining what the goal is and how to achieve that goal is one of the tasks that the office manager will be required to perform.

2. **Organizing** – Office managers will be responsible for the overall organization of the office and in most cases will be the central point of contact for everything having to do with the day to day running of the office. Some examples of things that they might be asked to organize include: daily/weekly/monthly meetings, performance reviews, when personnel will be on vacation, and assignment of tasks to team members.

3. **Teaming** – The ultimate job of hiring and firing is usually left to the doctor, however recruiting candidates and gathering resumes for job openings, selecting potential candidates, training, and reprimanding unacceptable behavior is usually is taken care of by the office manager.

4. **Leadership** – ability to influence others to perform tasks; this includes setting defined tasks and goals and encouraging the team to achieve desired results.

5. **Controlling/Monitoring** – ensuring that everything flows effortlessly and the daily journey is set toward achieving the goals of the practice.

The skills needed to accomplish these tasks include:

- ✓ **Good communication** – both verbal and written
- ✓ **Good listening** – you must always be receptive to what people are telling you. Taking the time to listen will pay huge dividends and can save an office manager from making grave mistakes
- ✓ **Good leadership** – lead by example; motivate for results, know your office team and what motivates each of them, what works on one person will not necessarily work on another

- ✓ **Tolerance for diversity** – understanding that all of us are not the same and everyone works differently
- ✓ **Being Proactive** – looking to the future, don't get caught up just 'fighting the alligator closest to the boat'
- ✓ **Being Reactive** – able to handle situations on the 'fly' while making it look effortless, 'like a duck on the water'. On the surface nothing is moving but under the water their feet are propelling them forward

The bottom line is that as a leader, you have a responsibility to *affect* people in your office in a positive way, not *infect* people with negativity, arguing, gossiping and backstabbing. As a manager, you are always under the watchful eye of your team and you must lead by example.

WRITTEN COMMUNICATION

Written communication is very common in business situations, so it is crucial for small business owners and managers to develop effective written communication skills. Formatting and writing a business letter takes more time and preparation than any other type of communication but once you breakdown the format and get familiar with it, the process will become second nature to you. You must maintain the correct format in a formal letter, along with using correct grammar, spelling and tense. Take advantage of the tools at your fingertips.

Grammar and spelling can be easily checked with today's use of Microsoft Word. Take the time to heed all the warnings for grammar and spelling. After you write the letter, go back and reread it at least one more time for accurate content, tone, and the gotchas of properly spelled words that are not what you intended (example: there and their).

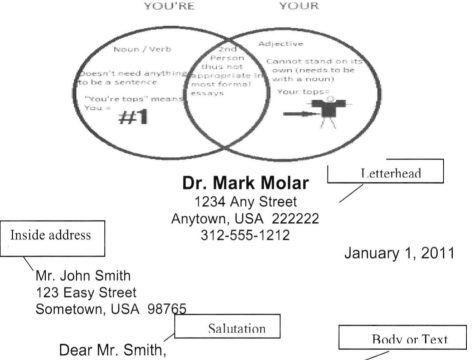

Dr. Mark Molar
1234 Any Street
Anytown, USA 222222
312-555-1212

January 1, 2011

Mr. John Smith
123 Easy Street
Sometown, USA 98765

Dear Mr. Smith,

This is the first line of the first paragraph. It should state the purpose of the letter or the reason for writing. This may be the only paragraph that gets read. Be brief and clear. Write and rewrite until you get it right.

This is the second paragraph, what most refer to as the body of the letter. Most letters have more than one

paragraph. Although your letter should be more exciting to read than this one, it will not be well received unless it has all of the essential elements of a standard business letter.

The last paragraph is the closing or concluding statement or point. This includes the final elements of the letter.

Sincerely,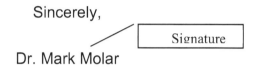

Dr. Mark Molar

T he parts of the letter include:

1. **Letterhead or typed heading** – the receiver of the letter needs to know who sent the letter and how to respond if necessary (envelopes are often separated from letters).
2. **Date** – if you take several days to complete the letter, use the date the letter is finished and ready to be signed out.

3. **Inside address** – it is not necessary to include the recipient's address, but if you do this is where it would go.
4. **Salutation** – This is the greeting; usually begins with Dear
5. **Body(Text)** – The body contains 3 parts
    - Beginning or opening statement
    - Main message
    - Conclusion or the 'wrap up'
6. **Complimentary closing** – usually it's 'Sincerely' or 'Regards'
7. **Signature** – The sender of the letter usually signs it
8. **Typed name** – due to the fact that the signature isn't always legible.

Line Spacing - In general, each element or paragraph of the letter is followed by a single blank line, except:

- The date, followed by three or four blank lines;
- The final content paragraph, followed by two blank lines;

- The valediction/closing, followed by three or four blank lines (enough for the sender to sign the letter); and
- The sender's title, followed by two blank lines.

Indentation Formats - There are generally 3 formats for business letters

- Block – all text is aligned to the left margin with no indentions and the paragraphs are either double or triple spaced.
- Semi-block – all text is aligned to the left margin and paragraphs are indented, usually with 5 spaces.
- Modified Semi-block - all text is aligned to the left margin, except for the author's address, date and closing are all indented at least 3 spaces (they must all be matched) and all paragraphs are indented 5 spaces.

Additional examples of Business letters:

Email, memos and other forms of written communication may not be as formal as an actual letter but certain things need to remain consistent. Your meaning must be concise and to the point; you must always be courteous, tactful and professional, even if to a 'friend'. Remember that the written word can be misunderstood, because there are no inflections in the voice to emphasis certain points.

The nice thing about written communication is that it can be edited and revised several times before being sent so that the content can be shaped to achieve the maximum effect, which is important because it will also provide a permanent record of the messages that have been sent and can be saved for later.

The bottom line here is to read, reread and then read it again before you send it. On your last review, look at it from the recipients point of view. How will it be received and

perceived? Be careful, cautious and professional at all times because anything in writing can be considered a legal document and therefore binding. Finally, always assume it will be shared with others and temper what you write accordingly!

VERBAL COMMUNICATION

Verbal communication is the unwritten form of communication. Whether you are the one doing the talking, or the one listening, mere words are not the only thing in play here. Body language, facial expressions and the eyes tell so much about the message being conveyed.

Some key things to remember when engaged in verbal communication are:

- Use positive words and gestures

- Think before you speak; know what you are going to say and speak your thoughts clearly and concisely
- Avoid profanity at all costs
- Ask questions if in doubt
- Allow the speaker to finish a thought without interruption
- Let the other person know you are listening to them, possibly by repeating back part of what they said.

Missing the meaning
By Denise Ciardello

Facial expressions are valuable tools when one human is communicating with another. Raised eyebrows show surprise, an open mouth and eyes signify disbelief, and a wink can convey flirting or pulling one's leg. When you are face to face with someone, sometimes you can tell someone doesn't quite get your point because they are squinting their eyes and/or a furrowed brow indicates that the person is thinking (or that the sun is shining brightly!). Besides facial expressions most people also exhibit body language. Arms crossed over the chest could mean the person is closed to what you are saying, bored, mad, or possibly just cold, but you can't really tell without also looking at the face. Applause is typically an outward symbol of approval; however, if the clapping is performed slowly with a sneer on the face, it is obviously meant as a sarcastic gesture. Another valuable tool when communicating is verbal language, yet that too needs more than words for full understanding. When a sentence is spoken, emphasis is placed on certain words or phrases and that adds meaning to the statement. As an example, take the following question: "What is your name?" Say it out loud four times and each time put the accent on a different word within the sentence. Do you see how the meaning changes each time? Now add in facial expressions and body language and you can determine if it's just an information gathering question or if the inquirer is mad, frustrated, or being sarcastic. If it takes all these visual and verbal signs to understand the meaning of a simple question, how can we possibly communicate effectively with mere written words? In informal written communication (mainly e-mail and texting) people have devised a method by developing symbols, or emoticons, to help us express our meaning a bit more clearly.

For instance, :) is a smile. Other electronic emotions include: :(frown, :-P playful/silly <3 love, ;) winking (Ironically, a 20-something was heard recently stating that he didn't know that the semicolon had a purpose except for making a wink.)

How many times has the meaning of a sentence or even an entire e-mail been misinterpreted because there were no facial expressions to decipher, or body language to assist with the connotation? Emoticons can help convey meaning when e-mailing, but are they enough? Keep in mind also that if the e-mail is being read on a mobile device, many times the emoticon many not show up properly, if at all. Emotions are contagious. We communicate in many ways, not just with words but also with facial expressions, body language, and the tone in our voices. Have you ever experienced the change in someone's attitude, simply by sharing a smile? One person may comfort another at a sad time with a gentle pat on the shoulder and a sympathetic look; a calm voice and a genuine smile may be the exact emotion needed to diffuse anger or frustration.

Can those things truly be accomplished with a simple emoticon? A thought is being typed by one person, yet the receiver of the thought may be emphasizing a different word in the sentence, thereby giving it an entirely new implication, possibly sarcasm (:-7) or worse.

It is important to remember that in our fast and furious lifestyle, our words are not always read in the same tone that they were written. This is especially significant when writing to someone we do not know very well or with a business dealing. Although we do not think we have the time, picking up the phone may be just what is needed to allow someone to receive your true, genuine intent. Words are very powerful in written or spoken form and emotions are the way we send and receive the words properly. On the flip side, when sending an e-mail or text, we have the ability to erase words before they are sent. Rereading is priceless and always recommended. Remember, once you throw that stone, you can never take it back.

Article published in DentistryIQ 7-23-2010

Marketing

There are two different types of marketing that will be used in your practice;

Internal and **External**. Internal marketing is an ongoing process that occurs strictly within a practice whereby the functional process aligns, motivates, and empowers employees at all levels to consistently deliver a satisfying customer experience.

That means that you market within your practice, which consists of asking patients for referrals, giving them the exceptional care that they expect, sending them thank you notes and extra recognition when they refer friends and family.

External marketing is the ongoing process that occurs outside a practice for promotional purposes. This includes any and all advertising that is placed in a newspaper, magazine, newsletter, website, billboard or anything that is outside the walls of your office. To maximize your return, each activity should be scrutinized to determine if they complement, overlap, or simply don't deliver.

Internal Marketing

The first step to good internal marketing is exceptional customer service, which in the dental office translates to great patient care. If you are delivering outstanding patient care, your patients are going to tell 2 friends (or family), who will tell 2 friends, who tell 2 friends, etc. to come to your office. So what is  outstanding service? Taking good x-rays? Providing a good cleaning? Making sure the crown you deliver has perfect margins?

These are good dental care steps; but outstanding service goes beyond this and is how you treat the patient as a person. You want to make sure everyone that walks through the door knows that they are important to you; greet them by name, listen to their every need and make them feel as though you came to work today just to make that person's experience in your office a great one. This could include offering a bottle of water, asking about their kids, **BEING ON TIME!**

Following their visit, send thank you notes, especially after a new patient visit. Consider having the entire team sign the card. You will want to thank your patients for the referrals that they have sent to you. If you have a patient that has sent several referrals to you, you may want to do something very special, such as sending flowers or an edible arrangement to the patient's place of work. What a great way to advertise!

Do you have to treat every patient this special? YOU BET! That's outstanding customer service.

You want your patients talking about the service they received in your office. If they are not talking about good service, then they are talking about bad

service.

If you provide bad service to a patient, they will tell everyone they know, who will then tell 2 people, who will tell 2 people, etc. Get the point?

The difference between bad service and outstanding service is relative, and the patient is the judge and jury, when determining the difference. How do you know when you are providing outstanding customer service? You merely have to answer one little question: Is this how I would want to be treated?

So what about THAT patient? You know which one we're talking  about. Every office has at least one. Nothing makes THAT patient happy.

The morning huddle is about how to get THAT patient out without a scene being caused. The answer is YES; even THAT patient needs to have outstanding customer service. In your huddle, challenge the office to have that patient leave with a smile. It's important because THAT patient will not tell 2 people – that patient will tell everyone he/she comes in contact with about your office; standing in line in the grocery store, waiting for the dry cleaning, as their gas is being pumped.

If that difficult patient is talking, you need to do everything you can to make sure it is about the outstanding service that you provided. Everything inside the practice is about your internal marketing campaign, so make sure that the wall hangings, décor and paint on the walls is what you want to portray to your patients. When was the last time you sat in one or all of the operatory chairs to see what your patients see or listened to the sounds, conversations and noises that occur in your office? Pretend you are a patient and evaluate your office from the moment you get out of your car to walking out of the front door. This is a great exercise for everyone on your team.

Would you LIKE me?

By Christopher Ciardello

Facebook is a social media outlet that most Americans are familiar with; even people who don't have a Facebook profile have their fair share of knowledge of its increasing importance in our society. In the past couple of years Facebook developed what are called Facebook Pages; these Pages are created by someone with a Facebook account that wants to promote a business or event. Having a Facebook Page for your office today is as important as having a yellow pages ad 10 years ago because can help increase the traffic into your office. Let's discover a few things about this new/old phenomena and what it takes to create a Facebook page and then to maintain it.

The first thought that comes to mind when Facebook is mention is probably that it is an outlet for the kids to stay in touch with each other. You've heard that they put any and everything on their profile. It's a social thing so why do you want to bring it into your business? For one thing, it's not just for kids – most adults have a Facebook profile now. And it is a social thing, and that is exactly why you want to bring it into your business. People talk about everything on their profiles from where they went on their vacation to the restaurant they are eating at right now. Businesses can allow people to 'check in' which tells the world where they are at that very minute. How cool would it be if your patients told all their friends that they just checked into your practice? You can't pay for a more effective form of advertising. The largest referral source you have at your fingertips is word of mouth –viola'…..Facebook. Patients who are referred to your office by a friend are much more likely to stay with your office for the long haul.

Creating and maintaining a Facebook Page can be seem intimidating, and yet you probably already have the best resource for this part right in your office. Any team member you have that is under the age of 35 can handle this task, because they were born with a microchip in their brain and know Facebook better than they know the back of their hand. Having frequent activity on your Page can help your patients feel connected to your office and encourages them to tell their friends about your office. Your team member would be in charge of posting statuses, pictures, fun quotes,

specials going on in the office and/or tips for good oral hygiene. It makes it more fun if everyone on the team contributes something for the posts.

The owner of the business should be the creator of the Facebook Page through their Facebook account. Once you have created the Facebook Page you can add multiple people to the administrative rights. The owner should start the page because they have the rights to add and delete people from the administrative rights. This is a safety measure just in case, heaven forbid, a disgruntled employee quits and has the ultimate rights to the Facebook Page. This employee could keep the owner from having access to the Facebook Page and severely hurt the practice's reputation. If you find that you need help setting this up, we can help you with that.

Once you get your page up and running, send out a newsletter with a link to your Facebook Page asking your

patients to "Like" you. Every time a patient likes your Page, Facebook posts a status to all the friends of that patients' newsfeed; notifying them that they like your office. The more people "Like" your Page, the more traffic that will be generated. This is important because the more traffic you have going through your Facebook Page, helps to boost your online presence, which leads more new patients to find you on the web.

There are some rules and regulations to make sure you follow for your Facebook Page. Such as:

- You cannot offer prizes or gifts to people to "Like" your page; they have to "Like" it on their own free will.

- If you do offer deals on your Facebook Page, all restrictions must be disclosed on your Page.

- You also cannot use the "Like" function as a voting mechanism for a promotion.

- You can have a random drawing of all the people that LIKE you during a certain time period, etc.

Read all the restrictions: Facebook.com/page_guidelines

Finally, you will want to set ground rules for whoever is in charge of this task. Limit the amount of time spent on maintaining and the content that can go on the Page. This is a form of marketing and as with all communication to the public; the owner will want to have final approval of information that is a direct representation of your practice.

We would love it if you would 'LIKE' us on Facebook/GlobalTeamSolutions.

External Marketing

There are several factors you want to consider before you decide what kind of external marketing you are going to use for the practice.

> **BUDGET** – marketing experts say that you should spend no less  than 1% of your monthly production on external marketing; what do you currently spend? Is it on a regular basis or do you wait until business slows down and you need it yesterday? It is recommended to put this in your monthly budget. Make it a regular process, just like sending out those recall reminders.

> **TARGET AUDIENCE** – who is your patient? If you work primarily on children, do you want to market to the children or the parents? If your practice is primarily dentures, it may not be smart to advertise to young families. Remember that women make up 75% of the population that decides on where the family receives its dental services.

Market your office where you think your patients hang out. If you have family practice, consider sponsoring a local little league team and put the office name on the back of the kids' t-shirts. While the kids are running the bases, the moms, dads, aunts, uncles and grandparents will see "Dr. Molar's Family Practice" on the backs of their uniforms. If your services focus more toward cosmetic only, spend your marketing dollars where Lexus or Mercedes or other affluent companies advertise; if you have a practice for everyone Tom, Dick and Harry, then we go to where they are – the grocery store. Find out where your patients are hanging out and make your name visible there.

- **MATCHING THE MESSAGE** to your services – there are many ways to get your message to potential patients; billboards, postcards, radio, TV. Social media is the area that many dental offices are finding great success when it comes to marketing their office. It is where your patients are hanging out, whether it's on Facebook, Twitter, Instagram, LinkedIn, or Pinterest.

- **METHOD OF DELIVERY** – If you are a pedodontic office, day time dramas is probably not a good time to run a TV ad, yet the cartoon network might be a great alternative. February is dental health month and many schools and preschools welcome the opportunity to have dental professionals come into their classes for presentations. Email, texts and good old-fashioned postcards are great methods of delivery to get your name out to your patients of record, asking for referrals.

- **RETURN OF INVESTMENT (ROI)** - each new patient should have a referral source listed. Most practice management software has the ability to store that information and give a breakdown as to how much each referral source has brought in, production-wise. Make sure you ask!

Building credibility and achieving name recognition is the purpose for external marketing. Once you make these determinations, you can start your advertising. You can do press releases with the local paper; get involved in the community through schools, clubs, chamber of commerce and so on.

Review your website often and make changes whenever appropriate. This truly is one of the best ways to advertise. When you build your website, make sure that you optimize your site because this will leave a lasting impression with your current and prospective patients. If you do not know how to do this, get a contract with a professional IT person. You will only get one bite at the apple with most people, take advantage of it.

External marketing, along with your internal marketing, should be a routine process that is as common as brushing your teeth. Change things around if you determine you are not receiving as profitable an ROI as you would like. Discuss it in your team meetings and keep the ideas fresh and new. Remember that it may take some time to get the momentum going with any time of marketing process.

This is a team process. But wait, marketing is not my job, I just clean teeth. Although everyone in the office is skilled and trained on their particular areas of expertise, it is up to everyone to be on board with marketing of the practice; afterall patients are a requirement for remaining in business. It doesn't mean that you take turns standing on the street corner yelling about the wonderful services your practice offers; but it does mean that each team member carries and hands out office business cards. Telling friends, neighbors and family members about the wonderful, outstanding customer service that your office provides is a fabulous marketing tool. Marketing is truly a team thing.

Chapter 1 Recap

The job of a dental Office Manager is to maintain control over the dental office in many ways. The **Basic Functions** of any office manager include:

- Planning
- Organizing
- Teaming
- Leadership
- Controlling/Monitoring

Communication is used in every way for the office.

- ✓ Written communication – formal business letters, emails to patients and memos to team members;
- ✓ Verbal communication – which includes direction of tasks, and handling team disputes.
- ✓ Verbal means unwritten but it also includes body language, facial expressions and the eyes which tell so much about a message being conveyed.

Marketing is a crucial part of running any business. Two ways to promote a practice are Internal and external marketing. Both forms of marketing must always include the

practice's branding, along with a constant, concise message, to the correct audience.

What Does Your Welcome Mat *Sound* Like?
By Janice Janssen

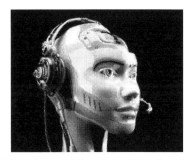

Recently, I found myself in the position of needing a new doctor. Like most people, this is not a task I enjoy, so I ask for a couple of referrals from my friends and began the daunting task of making phone calls to schedule an appointment. The first office I called, I was greeted by a very impersonal, robotic lady on the other line. I told her I would be a new patient and was looking to schedule an appointment. Her first question was what type of insurance I had and then they told me the first available appointment was in August. It may very well have been the first available new patient appointment at all in the practice…however, what lingered in my head was: 'Is that because of the insurance I have?' 'Could I have gotten in sooner if I had another insurance?' The phone call continued with the necessary questions: name, address, birthdate, etc. It was a very mechanical phone call that left me not caring whether I went to that office or not. The call did not necessarily discourage me from going, but I didn't care one way or the other. Indifference was the emotion I had when the call ended.

Since the office was not going to be able to get me in until August, I decided I would make another phone call to see if I could get in sooner somewhere else. A very nice gentleman with an English accent answered the phone --- he had me from Hello. I could tell immediately that this was the office for me. I explained to him, as I had to the first lady, that I would be a new patient coming to the practice. He asked which doctor I had been referred to...I told him...he said, *"OK, her first appointment available for a new patient is in July. If that works for you, I will get you scheduled with her. I also have a new doctor in the practice that has appointments available next week if*  *you would like to see her."* I wasn't sure what to do since I had been referred to the doctor with the next available appointment in July. This gentleman took the time to explain the new doctor's credentials, how long she'd practiced, and that she was a wonderful doctor. He felt sure that I would find her to be an awesome doctor. He talked her up so much that I decided to make the appointment for the next week. He then asked all of the pertinent questions.

There was a major difference as I hung up the phone this time. I now want, in fact can't wait, to go to this office. He was friendly, personable and seemed to have a genuine interest in me. I did not get to meet him at my appointment but I did tell the doctor that he sold me on coming to their practice. ☺

When was that last time that you talked up your doctor or hygienist to a new patient? The initial phone call is the most important marketing tool you have for your practice. It needs to be appealing and the patient needs to know that the office really has their best interest at heart. When a patient gets a robot on the phone that doesn't care whether they come to into the practice or not...chances are the patient will keep looking. Maybe they will look for an office that is closer, can get them in sooner, or takes their insurance, or even worse, just not show up. Whatever the case may be, make them WANT to come to your practice. Assure them that it is the place to be!

Chapter Two

PRODUCTIVE SCHEDULING

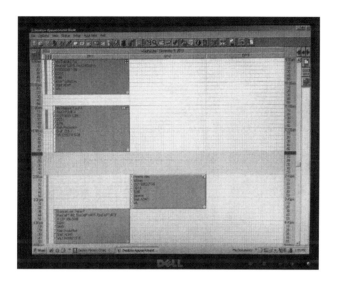

Scheduling appointments. It's easy. Just open the book, turn on the computer and start plopping in appointments, right? You don't want the doctor to see any 'holes' in the schedule so you simply plug in a patient wherever there is a hole. At the end of the day, you are exhausted from seeing a bunch of patients, only to find out that production was next to nothing.

Day after day, it seems as though you are marching in place. You, and your team are working your tails off but you are not making any headway toward achieving your office's goal. It can be a challenge to balance the need to keep the appointment book full and the desire to have every day be productive. Smart scheduling must be methodical and systematic.

Let's talk about simple techniques that will help you reach your goals without feeling exhausted at the end of the day.

1. **Block booking** is a technique that few offices will adhere to and yet those that do find the system incredibly liberating.

Block booking consists of:

- Just the right balance of High, Medium, & Low Production procedures so that you have a perfect day – everyday. Some offices refer to this as "Rock, Sand, and Water"; The Rock being the high production (crowns, bridges, etc.); the sand is your medium production (fillings, night guards, etc.); and water is your filler – low or non-productive procedures (crown seats, emergencies, etc.).
- Format for a routine day. In most practices, the highest production is scheduled at the beginning of the day. Your doctor will want to have a say in the formatting of the ideal day, so be sure to have this discussion before you set it up.
- There should also be time blocks for Scaling and Root Planning (SRP). Have you ever had SRP diagnosed but can't get the patient in for weeks because the hygienist is so fabulous at pre-appointing? That is not good for that perio patient that has recently been educated on the fact that he has periodontal disease and that he needs to take care of it right now.

➢ What about New Patients (NP)? Ideally, you want to have an appointment to offer a new patient within 48 hours of the initial phone call. This requires to have NP time blocks built into your schedule.

How many do you need? The easiest way to determine this is to take the average number of New Patients in a week and divide it by the number of days. If you, on average, have 16 NPs a month, that is 4/week and on a 4 day work week, that means you need one New Patient time block every day. It's as simple as doing the math.

*It's important to ensure that everyone holds fast to the time blocks. These are sacred times that are not to be ignored because a patient seemed like they needed to get in at that time. Keep the time block open and available until 24 or 48 hours (office preference) before the day.

If you HAVE to put that seat crown in at 8am, make sure that the 2 hour high production time block is met at another point in the day. Some practice management software will allow you to move the block. Remember to schedule approximately the same production each day so that the practice is well paced and that the doctor and the team can achieve a consistent day-in day-out workload.   (Figure1.1)

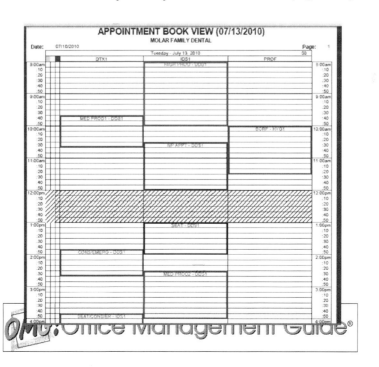

2. Set a daily goal – How do you know what you are working for if there is not a pre-determined goal? Even the greyhound knows that the goal is to catch the rabbit. The daily goal can be determined by either:

- Taking the percentage of the overhead that is met by the collection ratio; divide by 12 months; divide by 4 weeks and divide by the number of hours a week the office is open, or 40 if the team is paid on a 40 hour work week. Taking the monthly overhead for the practice and divide by the number of workdays in a month (some practices add a little for profit).

- Or by averaging the Dr's and the hygienist's last 3 monthly production totals; divide by the number of hours worked.

Whichever way your office decides to do it, set a daily goal and schedule to it. Every day, team members should know where they are toward their daily goal. Talk about it at each huddle. If there is a deficiency in the schedule in the future, mention it in the huddle so that each team member can keep that information close at hand and 'sell' it.

Emergencies or unscheduled treatment plans are perfect areas to use this information. "We would like to get you started as soon as we can find an opening in the schedule for you. We don't want to wait on this procedure."

3. **Linear vs. staggered booking** – Many offices feel that the doctor and assistant need to be in the same room all the time. This is a very inefficient scheduling system. When doctors and assistants are

scheduled correctly, practices see an immediate increase in efficiency. When you use the staggered booking method you will want to have a primary and secondary column. In the primary column, you are going to have about 70% of that time booked as doctor time. This will be the column for your higher production items. Your secondary column is about 30% doctor time. This is where you are going to schedule the low or no production procedures like cement crown, try-ins, etc. Refer to the example schedule (Figure 1.1) for questions on how to stagger the schedule.

4. **When to NOT double book** – The doctor can only be in one place at one time. It is impossible to have two consults beside each

other; by the same token, you have to remember that hygiene checks occur throughout the day also, so an appointment can't just be slapped into the schedule. We recommend that this conversation occur with the entire office – how does the Dr. want his/her schedule to be booked and when it is proper to have appointments scheduled beside each other. It is also the reason to bring tomorrow's schedule for everyone to review to try and alleviate future conflicts.

5. **Looking to the future** – The next two days are as important as today in terms of the appointment book. If there are any holes in hygiene, or the doctor's  schedule, make everyone in the office is aware of it.

Next week comes secondary to today, tomorrow and the next day. It's great to have a strong, complete schedule for next Thursday but you can pretty much guarantee it will change between now and then.

A practice's success depends on a strong scheduling system. Every practice has a schedule, but not all have a scheduling system. Smart scheduling should be methodical and systematic to keep the practice on goal.

6. **Handling Difficult Situations** – as much as you prepare, practice and prefer, you will still have difficult situations that occur when dealing with your patients. The number one thing to remember is to always remain professional and do not lose control of the situation. You've heard the saying 'make lemonade out of lemons'? When a patient calls to say they will

20 minutes late for their hygiene appointment, instead of rescheduling that patient, losing time and production encourage them to come on in. When the patient arrives, the hygienist will let him/her know that she will try to accomplish as much as possible. She may only get to the exam and x-rays, but at least some production was salvaged. The patient will be reappointed for the prophy appointment.

7. **Prime time appointment times** – these are usually the first and last appointments of the day. Just when you think you've done someone a favor by offering them a prime time appointment, they call to cancel at the last minute. To top it off, they want ANOTHER prime time. By explaining that this is a very sought after time slot and you do not have another 8am for 6 weeks, the patient may find a way

to make that appointment or will possibly reschedule at another time.

8. **Habitually late patients** – you may have a friend, sister or someone you know that is NEVER on time to anywhere. Every practice has a patient or two like this as well. You will want to document this so everyone is aware. You may opt to tell this patient that the appointment time is 20 or 30 minutes earlier than it actually is. If your practice routinely runs on time, explaining to the patient the need to be on time is essential.

9. **Drop-in or Walk-ins** - New patients are always welcome, right? If this is a brand new practice, a walk in might be a welcome sight, but most times scheduling another time for the patient to come in is required. If the patient has an emergency, it should be handled the same as if the patient called with an

emergency. Your practice may welcome walk-ins, which is why communication is very important to let the patient know that there may be a bit of a wait.

10. **Broken appointments** – What is your policy on broken appointments? You may choose to allow two per patient, after that put them on a same day appointment only list. You may want to charge a broken appointment fee. Whatever your office policy is, your patients need to aware of it. You will also want to document when and why a patient cancelled an appointment.

11. **Arriving on the wrong day** – This is one of the most uncomfortable times for the patient and the office. Sometimes it is convenient to see them that day; but most times it requires sending them away until the correct day. Handling the 'but your phone call stated that my appointment was today' is difficult. Be professional and respectful when dealing with the patient.

> "We shall never know all the good that a simple smile can do."
> Mother Teresa

---

2 Steps to Control Cancellations
By Chris Ciardello

There seems to be a common complaint when I go into offices these days; patients are cancelling the same day, or not giving the 24 hour notice that the office asks the patients to give. I typically follow up by asking if they are able to reschedule the patient and I usually hear 'yes, we try to get the patient back in as soon as possible'. Upon further examination, I'm discovering that patients are getting another appointment the next day, or later that week. It's time for a bit of "re-training" of the patients. This means that your patients need to understand that the doctor's and hygienist's schedule is valuable, and this can be accomplished by following a few important steps.

1. It begins when a patient calls to cancel their appointment – I find that there is not a real effort to save the appointment. The best way, I have found to save an appointment is to pause and then, with concern in your voice, say:

"Oh gosh, is there any way you can make this appointment? The doctor set aside this time just for you and was really looking forward to seeing you this morning/afternoon."

By having concern in your voice, you let the patient know that you are looking out for them by trying to save this appointment. You might remind them about your cancellation policy, in the event that there is a policy in place. If there is a fee that will be charged, it is advisable to have your patients know about this policy by giving them a copy of the cancellation policy and retaining a copy in their chart.

2. The second important step is determining when to schedule the patient. Often the team member will move the patients just a day or two out. This lets the patient know that its no problem to call last minute to cancel because they'll be able to get back on your schedule in a couple of days if something "better" pops up in their schedule. This prevents your patients from realizing that the doctor's time is precious to the office, and to other patients as well. In turn, if the doctor's schedule is full, there are not any appointments available in the near future.

Re-training your patients begins with the way that you respond to the cancellation call. If the patient is not able to make the appointment, then the standing rule is to push them out six weeks, regardless of the next available appointment. Even if tomorrow is wide open, six weeks is the rule for the next available appointment time otherwise you encourage the patient's behavior to cancel last minute. If you want your patients to respect the doctor's time, you need to respect the doctor's time as well. The conversation will go something like this:

"I'm so sorry that you can't make today's appointment. Dr. Molar's or Mary's (the hygienist's) next available appointment is _____." (state a date 6 weeks out)

"What? I can't wait that long; or my deductible is be due again by then; or I was hoping to have the work done before my daughter's wedding/my vacation / before school started."

"Oh I understand your dilemma, and that is why I was hoping you could make today's appointment."

This will be a wake up call to the patient that your time is valuable, and when the patient is baffled at the wait to get in the doctors schedule, let them know you can put them on the ASAP list and call them if there is a change in your schedule. The hardest part is to not yield to their demands that they need to come in sooner and that is just too far out. If they are trying to get you to find something earlier let them know that they can still come in for their original appointment but this is the next one available. Many times they will find a way to keep the original appointment. Other times, the patient may seem to get mad so it is important to remember that they are the ones that have chosen not to keep the appointment that they scheduled.

Once they have scheduled a new appointment and you have put them on the ASAP list, you can always call the patient back in a couple of hours and let them know about the opening in next week's schedule or whenever you do have an earlier time available. You might say something like:

"Mrs. Jones, I know that you were really wanting to come in sooner than _____, and I wanted to let you know that Mary has a change in her schedule for next Tuesday at 10:30am. Would you like for me to reserve that appointment for you?"

Nine times out of ten the patient will appreciate that you were looking out for them and more than likely take the earlier appointment.

This re-training will take some time to sink in for patients to start respecting your schedule, but I have seen this method work first hand! I have witnessed offices go from having 2-8 patients cancel/no show to having virtually no last minute cancellations. The hardest part is getting the admin team to stick with the rule; they see a hole in the schedule and want to fill it.

There are exceptions to every rule, like a patient's family member getting hurt, a car accident, and the patient coming down with the flu or some other contagious illness that no one wants spread around the office. You know your patients. You know which ones cancel for honest reasons, and which ones cancel because they don't feel like it, don't want to come in, or something more fun came up in their schedule.

Always ask the patient why they need to cancel their appointment and make sure to document it in their chart &/or on that appointment. Documenting their cancellations will help you to better understand if it's habitual or a true emergency. It should go without saying to always be respectful, never condescending to the patient. Be sympathetic and understanding, while also being firm and respecting your schedule. It's your schedule and you control it.

Article published in Dental Practice Management
November 15, 2014

Chapter 2 Recap

Scheduling is a very important task in the dental office. If the schedule is not full, then you are not meeting your production goals, and the doctor is not going to be happy.

Techniques to Scheduling:
- Block booking
    o The right balance of High, Medium and Low production procedures
    o Time blocks set aside for procedures such as scaling and root planing, crowns and new patients
- Setting your daily goal
    o Determine what your daily goal needs to be to meet the overhead of the practice
    o Schedule to it and discuss it in the daily morning huddles
- Linear and Staggered booking
- Double booking the provider
- Looking to the future-check the schedule in the next couple days to make sure it is scheduled to goal. If not, it is time to start calling patients to fill the schedule.
- Handling difficult situations
    o Handling prime time appointment cancellations

- Habitually late patients
- Drop-in or Walk-in patients
- Broken appointments
- Patients arriving on the wrong day

Chapter Three

OPTIMIZING INSURANCE SYSTEMS

We all hate the "I" word — **Insurance**. The mere mention of the word leads to eye rolls and heavy sighs. However just like paying taxes in life, to survive in the dental industry, your office will have to deal with the insurance world.

It doesn't matter if you are attached to big insurance by accepting all the plans, latched on by having primarily Medicaid patients, dipped your toe in the pool with only one or two plans, or are totally out of network yet still file and accept assignment of benefits from your patients' plans — it's a necessary evil that has crept into your practice.

What is the insurance aging system in your office? Is it non-existent except when you occasionally inquire about outstanding claims? Is it a chore that tears the flow of the office apart when it's "that time of the month"? Or is it a smooth, effortless occurrence that you never know even takes place, other than when you see the checks flowing in? The latter is what you need to achieve, and it

OMG! Office Management Guide®

is possible as long as the systems are in place to make it happen.

1. Verifying Insurance:

Do you verify insurance before seeing a patient? It constantly amazes us when we begin working with an office that does not verify insurance at all. Our immediately questions are:

- ❖ How do you know that patients have an insurance plan that will allow them to use their benefits in your office?

- ❖ How do you know they still have that particular plan?

- ❖ Do you think that an airline employee would let you on a flight and ask for your ticket at your destination?

- ❖ Or better yet, call you a month later and tell you that you were on the wrong flight?

- ❖ You arrived at your destination and received all the services you needed from the airline, so you would not be in a hurry to make amends on the outstanding bill, right?
  - ❖ Why would you let a patient come in for a cleaning, extraction, or crown and not know in advance how you will be paid?

Yes, this means that someone will have to call the Insurance company or go online to look up the benefits package. There are even companies that will do this for you at very reasonable rates. *(If you need assistance with finding these companies, please contact us.)*

When you have the patient on the phone to make an appointment, this is a great time to get their information. If this is an established patient, you will need to look for their insurance in the computer, or pull their chart to find it there, and verify that this is still their insurance and that there have not been any changes. If you have a new patient on the phone there are specific pieces of information that you will want to get. This will give you the ability to contact the insurance company prior to the patient's arrival. By handling it this way, there are no surprises when the patient comes in for that first appointment. You will not have to tell them they are not covered and possibly have to cancel or reschedule that appointment at the last minute because they do not want to have to pay out of pocket for your services.

Here is the information you will need to get from the patient:

1. Patient Name and Birth Date
2. Subscriber Name and Birth Date
3. Insurance Company Name
4. Insurance Phone Number

5. Subscriber ID or Social Security #
6. Subscriber's Employer and Group # on the card
7. Group Plan number or name

Once you have this information, you can call to verify the patient has coverage through this company. You will then want to get a break down of the benefits so you will know what their portion will be when they come in to your office.

Now that you have all the information you need, make sure you call the insurance for a breakdown of the patient's benefits.

> *To receive an* Insurance Benefits Verification Form, *email us at*
> **info@GTSgurus.com**

Insurance Benefits Verification Form

DENTAL INSURANCE VERIFICATION

Patient_____ Date_____ Staff Initials_____
Subscriber_____ Subscriber DOB_____ SSN_____-____-_____
Employer_____
Insurance Carrier _____Insurance Company Ph# (_____)_____-_____
Group #_____ Electronic Claims_____ Payor#_____
Do You Accept Assignment of Benefits?_____ Dependant coverage?_____
COB (Do you coordinate benefits?)_____Standard? _____ B'day rule _____Other?_____

        Insurance Representative's Name _____Time_____
        Mail Claim To:_____
        _____
        _____

Eligibility Date _____Plan Year = Calendar,___ Contract, _____ Other_____
Maximum Allowed_____ Benefits Used: _____Deductible Met? Ind_____ Family_____
Fees Based on UCR (Usual Customary and Reasonable)_____ Fee Schedule_____
Diagnostic/Preventive_____% Basic_____% Major_____% (*Indicates Deductible Applies)
Are there ANY waiting periods? _____If Yes, for what services_____
Eligible for Prosthetic Replacements_____ Pano_____ FMX_____ BWX_____Exam_____
Missing tooth clause? <u>Yes No</u> Endo- <u>Basic or Major</u>? Perio - <u>Basic or Major</u>? Oral Surg. - <u>Basic or Major</u>?
Are Buildups_____ Inlays_____ Onlays_____ Covered? 4355_____ basic/major ?
  Crns paid on prep / seat? Post Comp @ Ag fee ?_____
Ortho?_____ Maximum_____ Lifetime_____Deduct_____Info_____
Billing_____ Initial_____ Monthly_____Quarterly_____

History

☐ Last Prophy:_____ FMX:_____ Exam:_____ BWX: _____
☐ Can a Pano and FMX be covered at the same time? YES/NO

Prophy-Interval

☐ Do cleanings have to be **exactly** 6 months apart? YES / NO
☐ Does a patient have to go through periodontal surgery before having more than 2 prophies per year? YES / NO
☐ Can the Hygienist scale more than one quadrant per visit? YES / NO   Frequency ____

Flouride

☐ Is Adult Flouride Covered? YES / NO   Number of times per year_____
☐ Is Child flouride covered?   YES / NO   Number of times per year_____
  Sealants?_____

Denise Ciardello   www.GTSgurus.com   Janice Janssen
210-862-9445   314-644-8424

When contacting the insurance company, sometimes you might be able to go through the insurance's automated system and get all of the information you need; or you may be able to get a fax back from the insurance company that will give you all their information; other times, you are going to have to get a live person to answer your questions.

The idea of this verification form is that you have all of the questions you need at your fingertips and you just have to fill it in as you go. After you get the information, use this form to enter all of their information into your computer and you are ready for this patient to come in and get their services completed. Using this information, you can give them a pretty close estimate of what they are going to need to pay and what their insurance will cover.

Keep in mind when talking to the patient that what you tell them the insurance is going to pay is **only an estimate.** We never want to  give a guarantee; insurance companies are fickle and may deny the claim for some unforeseen reason. NEVER make that promise! You do not want the patient holding you responsible if the insurance does not pay. Also remember: you are doing the patient a favor by submitting the insurance and handling that part for them. **The contract is between the patient and the insurance company, not your office.** (The only caveat to this is if the insurance company is a PPO that you are contracted with—it is in your contract that you will submit the insurance claim for their patients)

Here is a breakout of certain sections with explanations of the information you are requesting and why:

- ✓ The deductible is important so you can let the patient know how much is due before they have benefits available to them for treatment.

- ✓ You will also find out their effective date, which is when they began their benefits.

- ✓ The yearly maximum is the MOST that their insurance is going to pay in the calendar, or their fiscal year.

- ✓ Waiting periods - some insurance companies will not pay out some benefits until the patient has had their coverage for an allotted amount of time.

- ✓ The final question is whether there is a missing tooth clause. If the answer is "Yes", the insurance will not pay for any service that is replacing a tooth that was removed prior to their coverage, basically an existing condition.

In the next section you are going to check on the percentage that they will cover on Preventative, Basic and Major services. The general breakdown was usually 100-80-50, but that has been changing over the years. The Y/N is to indicate if the deductible needs to be applied to these services.

You will then break it all down and ask the questions as you go:

What % do they cover on x-rays; extractions; surgical extractions; etc? Sometimes they will cover all of these at different percentages so in order to get our estimates right for the patient we need to know all of this information. Where it says:

Repl Y/N, this is asking if they will replace a partial, denture, bridge, etc. and if the answer is yes, then the next question is "How old does the prosthetic have to be to qualify for replacement?" The last question that needs some clarification is "Amalgam benefit for post comp?" Some insurance will not cover posterior composites but will down grade them and pay at an amalgam price.

Prevent % Y / N	**Basic** % Y / N	**Major** % Y / N
X-rays____% Y / N	Simple Ext ___%	Repl Y/N___Yrs
Sealants__%SurgExt_%		OcclGuard _%
To age_____	Endo _____%	
1x per ____yrs	Perio _____%	
Molars / Bicuspids	Perio Maint____%	
Debride___%	Amalgam benefit for post comp? Y/N	

Our next section has to deal with frequency limitations. The insurance companies are very particular about how much time has elapsed between some of the procedures we provide. If they say a prophy is every 6 months, you need to schedule that patient's appointment at **6 months + 1 day**.

Frequency

Prophy: 1x / Cal Yr -- 2x /Cal Yr -- 1x / 6 mos--1x / 12 mos
BWX : 1x / Cal Yr -- 2x /Cal Yr -- 1x /6 mos --1x / 12 mos
Fluoride: 1x /Cal Yr -- 2x / Cal Yr --1x /6 mos --1x /12 mos
Age _____
Pan / FMX: 1x per ___Date of last Pan / FMX _____

In the final section you are finding out if the patient has any orthodontic coverage. Obviously, you will not need this if your office does not do orthodontics. Finally you want to know if this insurance company is on a payment schedule. This means that the insurance does not pay on a percentage, they will just pay a set fee.

For example: For a prophy code they will pay a total of $45 instead of 100% of your fee. If they do pay on a Payment Schedule you will want to ask them to fax it or send it to you so you will be able to give your patients the best estimate you can on their insurance benefits.

ORTHO Coverage? Y/N To Age_____ Max $_____
Deductible: _____
Payment schedule _____
Verified by_____ Ins. Rep's Name_____ Date_____

Alright! You are done. You have just verified insurance benefits for your patient. Depending on the practice you work in, you are either going to file this sheet in the patient's chart or enter the information in to the computer.

INSURANCE VERIFICATION WORKSHEET

Patient: **John Smith**
Procedures: Comp Exam $53, FMX $85, Px Adult $61

Total Fee: $_____

Deductible $_____

Coverage %_____

Insurance Benefit $_____

Patient Portion $_____

Patient: **Mary Jones**

Procedures: Porcelain Crown #14 $1200

Total Fee: $_____

Deductible $_____

Coverage %_____

Insurance Benefit $_____

Patient Portion $_____

Patient: **Donald Garcia**

Procedures: One-Surface Posterior Composite #3 O

Total Fee: $_____

Deductible $_____

Coverage %_____

Insurance Benefit $_____

Patient Portion $_____

Finally, there are a few different types of insurance and you need to be familiar with what is out there, as well as a couple of rules when filing secondary insurance.

2. Types of Insurance Coverage

- **Traditional or Fee for Service**—this type will pay off of your Usual and Customary (UCR) fees. So you charge your fees and they will pay the percentage that they tell you when you call to verify.

- **Preferred Provider Organization (PPO)**—this is an insurance plan that you can either opt-in to their network or not. If you are a preferred provider then you are agreeing to accept the insurance company's fees and then they will pay the percentage off of their fees. **You cannot charge any higher than their fees**. If you are an out-of-network provider, the patient can still see you, but you will charge your UCR fees and the patient will have to pay the difference between the two.

- ❖ **Health Maintenance Organization (HMO)**—with this type of plan the patient has to choose a doctor that is in-network. **They will not receive any benefits if you are out-of-network.** If you decide to be an in-network provider with any HMO plans, they will pay you a flat rate per patient. It does not matter how many times they come in, or what they have done while under your care.

- ❖ **Medicaid**—this plan is through the government. You have to be a participating provider for the patients to be able to have services in your office; however Medicaid does pay for most procedures that is done in your office. Be aware that what you will be paid (and all you can accept) is a much lower amount than what your normal fees would be.

Secondary Insurance

What do you need to know when a patient has secondary insurance? Doesn't it just pick up what the primary didn't pay? Unfortunately, it does not all the time. Here are a few things you will need to know when dealing with a patient's secondary insurance:

> **The Birthday Rule**—when calling the insurance companies of patients with double coverage you will need to ask **BOTH** of the companies whether they abide by the birthday rule. This rule states that the subscriber that has their birthday EARLIEST in the year is the primary insurance company. The year the subscriber was born does not have any relevance, just the month and date.

> **Coordination of Benefits (COB)** - you will also want to ask the secondary insurance if they use COB. If they say yes, it means that if the primary pays 80% and that is what the secondary would pay, **then the secondary is not going to pay anything**. If the primary only covers 50% and the secondary would cover 80%, then the secondary will pick up the other 30% that the primary would not cover.

3. Claim Submission:

How do you submit claims to the insurance company? Are you still printing and sending your claims by snail mail? If you have even one working computer in your office, you have the technology, so why aren't you using it? Electronic claims are not just the way of the future; they are the way of today. It is a proven fact that you will receive payment on your claims twice as fast with an electronic submission.

That should be reason enough to find an electronic process and use it. The best part about electronic claims is that each time you send a batch of claims; you receive a status report on previously sent claims. This gives you a sneak preview of what the EOB will look like before that paper comes in the mail. If an X-ray or any additional documentation is needed, you will know sooner and get to it quicker, which allows you to get paid in a more expeditious manner.

This leads to the issue of submitting X-rays with the claims. Yes, there are still some insurance companies that do not accept electronic attachments, but those numbers are dwindling every day ... OK, every year.

The electronic clearinghouse that you use will give you details on how to begin this process and the percentage of companies that accept them. Without a doubt it is worth the phone call. If your radiography process has not come into the digital age, then you still must send a copy of the X-ray, print the claim, and send it through the good ol' U.S. mail system.

Remember to send a copy, and DO NOT send the originals. Most insurance companies no longer return X-rays. Your prophy, perio maintenance, fillings, etc., may still go electronically. Now that we have streamlined the submission process, let's move on to the aging of claims.

3. Insurance Aging: How often do you work on insurance aging? These are your claims that are overdue. Possibly the first question is: When do you consider a claim overdue? Industry and insurance standards dictate 30 days; however, if you use the electronic

claims process, this number should be decreased to 20 days. Is your insurance

aging report run daily, weekly, or monthly? How much is too much or not enough?

By running your report monthly, you are probably increasing the delay in payment from the insurance company. Think of it this way — you submit a claim for Mr. Smith on May 10, and you typically work your outstanding claims on the 20th of each month, so by June 20 when Mr. Smith's claim isn't paid you contact the insurance company (you are now at 40 days past the DOS), only to find out that the claim was never received and you must resubmit it.

Using your current method, it will be 70 days before you "revisit" this claim. In our professional opinion, doing this monthly is not efficient and you are leaving your money in the hands of the insurance company, instead of in your bank account.

Some insurance coordinators run their insurance reports daily. This may be overkill, but we applaud their aggressiveness and tenacity. These are the offices that typically have only one or two claims over 30 days. Hurray for those go-getters!

Our experience has proven that this should be on your weekly task list. You catch the "non-received" and the "additional information needed" more quickly and get paid in a more timely manner. We previously mentioned the status reports with electronic claims, and if those are being monitored you will catch the claims that require additional information in short order. In this case the weekly report will assist you with the claims that were never received. Side note:

Doesn't it seem like every fifth claim is never received?

4. Tracking outstanding claims: How are you documenting your conversations with the insurance companies? We will go back to the first point of this chapter, if you have computers and are filing electronically, documentation should be maintained on your computer. Most practice management software has an "insurance status" box, window, or notes section. Use your software to benefit you and those that might be coming in behind you.

It's incredibly frustrating to see members of the same team put notes in different places — some on the computer, some on the paper report, and others on sticky notes. Set up a system for your office and train all team members on the system (please don't use sticky notes; this is a recipe for disaster).

What should you document? The person's name (which gives you credibility if you have to call back), the date and time, what was discussed and the course of action agreed upon. If the claim had to be resubmitted, document that. If the representative told you the claim would be processed within 10 days, write it down in a place that will remind you to call and check on it in 11 days. You must follow up because the odds are that they will forget about you with the click of the receiver.

5. Insurance Payments: How do you input your payments? Say for example someone paid for only three of the four procedures submitted. How do you resubmit that part of the claim?

Some versions of practice management software allow you to split the primary claim so you can satisfy part of it with the payment and resubmit the unpaid procedures. Or, you get the check and life is good. But wait, the estimate you gave the patient for their portion was WAY off and the person now has a large balance.

You may need to do some research to determine if additional appeals need to be made; whatever the outcome, don't forget to document your findings. If the balance is truly the patient's to pay, drop a statement in the mail instead of waiting until you run statements at the end of the month.

This way when the patient calls you in two days to inquire about the balance, it's still fresh in your mind and you can explain the reason. Another method of payment to consider is direct deposit. Talk about the speed of lightening. You will receive payments two to three times faster than with conventional methods.

We also recommend appealing any procedure that is denied unless it is due to benefits maxing out or it is a non-covered benefit. Most denials are never appealed yet those that are appealed typically will get paid. It's worth a try –restate your reason for the procedure and resubmit.

What are your insurance systems? Are they being followed? Are you happy with the results? Industry standards state that .5% to 1% of your monthly production is acceptable as outstanding insurance A/R. Any more than that and you are letting someone else hang on to your money — interest free. Not a very profitable savings plan. This is money that is rightfully yours and should be in your pocket.

All dental offices have to deal with insurance companies in one way or another. Spending time setting up the proper systems for verifying, submitting, and working the insurance aging report can change insurance companies from the beasts that you dread tangling with into manageable tasks that keep the cash flowing. In addition, your patients will appreciate the fact that you stay on top of their benefits and payments.

"Whatever you are, be a good one."
Abraham Lincoln

---

3 Steps for Efficient Insurance Systems

By Denise Ciardello

You have a healthy number of patients coming through the door but it seems as though the collections are not keeping up with production. The insurance companies are delaying payments on everything from crowns to fillings, which makes collecting on claims more difficult than ever. What is the secret to faster claim processing?

The secret is that the insurance companies do not want to pay on claims. Well, that's a big DUH! The true secret to is have insurance systems put in place which will keep the collection ratio at a manageable state. This can be broken into 3 steps and if followed correctly, will decrease the processing time of most claims.

1- Send the claim correctly the 1st time. Don't laugh! It happens all the time – sending off the claim with fingers crossed or even insurance coordinators that try to 'fight' the system by not sending x-rays or other information until it is requested. Who is that really hurting? Most electronic claims clearing houses will warn you if an insurance company requires additional information for specific procedures. It's advisable to heed the warnings. Here are some tips for proper claim submission:

· Verify that you are sending the claim to the right place. The patient telling you is not verification. Whether you use the insurance company's website, a verification service or

pick up the phone and call, make sure that you are sending the claim to the right place. Crossing your fingers and hoping it's right is NOT a good plan. In the words of Ronald Reagan "Trust but verify".

- *As a rule of thumb, send x-rays on all crowns, implants, root canals (pre & post) and scaling & root planning.*
- *SRP will also require a perio chart.*
- *Narratives need to accompany major treatment – this information should be in the clinical notes for ease of accessibility. When putting the narrative on a claim, remember that only 150 character spaces will be submitted electronically in 'Remarks for Unusual Services' box. Keep a list handy of narratives that your doctor uses frequently.*
- *For all crowns, document if it is an initial or replacement crown; there is a box on the claim form for this information. Even non-clinical people can determine that by looking at the x-ray. If it is a replacement crown, what is the date of the initial placement? This is the tricky part. You are not allowed to 'guess' or make up a date. If the initial crown was not completed in your office, you need to ask the patient how long he/she has had the crown. By explaining to*

the patient that their insurance will not pay on the crown unless you give a date of the initial

· Finally, there are insurance companies, like Cigna, that will only pay on a crown, the patient is more likely to work with you. You may need to jog their memory by asking questions (Were you married? How old was your child? Was it before 2000?)

Ideally this information should be included in the clinical notes, so make it part of the clinical notes template. crown once the permanent crown is seated. Again, keep track of that so you can submit that information as soon as it occurs. We recommend that you document it on the 'crown seat' appointment. Many times they will accept the seat date over the phone and will send the claim on for final processing.

2- Track outstanding claims on a weekly basis. We often see Insurance Aging reports that have several pages – the most we've seen is 58, but have heard of reports with hundreds of pages. This is a system that needs to be worked often and with purpose. The longer the report, the more overwhelming it is to get a handle on it.

Clearing houses will usually send a status report following the submission of claims. These reports have valuable information on them so take a minute to look them over each day. Words like 'unprocessed', 'holding', 'zero pay' or 'rejected' should get your attention. You can do the research and find out why the claim is not being processed to your satisfaction. By waiting until the Explanation of Benefits (EOB) comes in the mail, you are typically 30 days into the life of the claim.

The insurance websites are also a great source of information for tracking outstanding claims. Sites like Metlife give you full details and although the others are as user friendly, they still have valuable information.

Lastly, appeal – appeal – APEAL! If a procedure is denied that you feel should be paid, send it back for reprocessing; this includes crown build-ups that 'are part of the crown prep procedure'. Explain why you are appealing it through a more detailed narrative. Your Dr. or hygienist can help with these details.

Statistics show that 85% of all denied procedures are not appealed. Of the 15% that are appealed, 75% are reprocessed with a payment. The odds are in your

3- Consider using the Direct Deposit. Most insurance companies will allow you to sign up for electronic transfer of funds to the practice's bank account. This alleviates checks lost in the mail or waiting on snail mail to deliver the check.

You are notified by email or fax (your choice) which claims have been processed, then the payment is inputted by getting the information from the website. The absolute best part is the speed of payment. Hygiene claims can be processed in 2 days and treatment claims, including crowns, will sometimes have the money in the bank within a week.

Insurance companies are not fun to deal with but they have become the norm in most dental practices. Learning to work with them so that the money is collected quickly is imperative. Don't let your money remain on their side of the fence any longer than it needs to be. This is the easy money. Have good, consistent insurance systems in place and your collections will remain in line with your production.

Article as published Dentistry IQ
July 2013

Chapter 3 Recap

Remember, when dealing with insurance, it is crucial to set up good systems.

First and foremost - verify! Verify! **VERIFY!** The same information needs to be gathered every time. You can use the form provided or customize your own.

Understand the different types of **insurance plans** out there:

- ❖ Traditional or Fee For Service
- ❖ Preferred Provider Organization (PPO)
- ❖ Health Maintenance Organization (HMO)
- ❖ Medicaid
- ❖ Secondary Insurance

Claim submission – are you sending claims through the mail or electronically?

Insurance aging – when do you consider a claim overdue? How do you keep **Track of Insurance claims**?

Insurance Payments – are you inputting them correctly?

The answers to these questions and more are key points to creating, implementing and sustaining effective and efficient insurance systems.

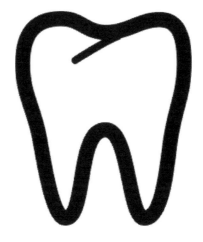

Chapter Four

THE BASICS OF
MEDICAL CROSS-CODING

Something that is fairly new in the dental office and one that not many dental offices are utilizing is billing dental claims to a patient's medical insurance. You cannot send all claims to medical insurance, but there are some you can.

Utilizing a patient's medical insurance whenever possible is a great benefit to the patient and to the office itself. With dental insurance still having the same $1000-$2000 maximums that they have had for at least the last 30 years, you cannot get a lot of benefit for the patient simply out of their dental insurance. That being said, it is time for you to learn how to maximize your patients' benefits!

Services that are Billable to Medical Insurance:

- Trauma-related procedures
    - This catchall takes in anything that happened as the result of an accident
- Appliances

- Sleep Apnea
- TMD
- Screenings
  - Oral Cancer
  - Saliva Testing (HPV, Acidity Levels, etc.)
- Procedures associated with Systemic Conditions
  - Periodontal
  - Implants
  - Oral Surgery
  - These services can be covered if there is a medical necessity for the procedure

Trauma related procedures are always covered by medical insurance and should be billed there first. When a trauma patient comes in you will need to get the correct information. Many times we just whisk them back to the operatory and get to work.

Now of course we need to be in a rush...they are in pain and need immediate attention. Therefore, when that patient calls to tell you they are coming in, tell them to bring their medical card. This way they will probably have it out and ready when they walk in the door.

While the patient is back in the operatory, the insurance coordinator can call the insurance company. Make sure to get the correct mailing address. Then you will need to have the patient fill out a questionnaire that will ask the most commonly asked questions by medical insurance companies. One of these forms is available for you on the next page. This will give the insurance company the information they need about the accident to process the claim.

It is also important to remind your patients as you do with dental insurance, that their insurance policy (whether medical or dental) is a contract between the patient and their Insurance—you are not a party to that. Even if you code your procedures appropriately, some claims may not be covered by the patient's insurance policy.

Accident Report

Patient'sName: ___ Today's Date: ____

Date of Accident: _____ Time of Accident: __

Place of Accident: _____

Type of Accident:

Auto: Was patient Driver or Passenger?_____

Fall: Did you fall from one level to another or slip/trip?_____

Sports injury? Work-related? Hit by blunt force?

Was there a police or emergency room report? Y / N

Describe the Accident in Detail:

Have you sought other medical attention for this accident? Y / N

If so, by whom? _____

What body parts were injured in this accident? _____

Describe the pain at the time of the accident

Alright, you now know WHAT you can bill to the medical insurance. Now how are you going to do it? First of all, you want to make sure you have all of the information needed. You are going to get a copy of the medical insurance card and call the insurance company, just like you do for dental insurance.

There are fewer questions that will need to be asked however. The next page has a verification form for the medical insurance. Using this form will ensure that you get the same information every time you call.

Medical Necessity

A procedure is NOT going to be covered by the medical insurance unless it is deemed medically necessary. Here is the question you have to ask yourself: "Is the procedure appropriate to the evaluation and treatment of a disease, condition, illness or injury?" If the answer is YES then you can send in a claim to the patient's medical insurance. If NO then there will not be any benefit. Basically, you are saying that in order to get the patient to a "healthy state" these procedures are necessary. This is why for trauma-related procedures you can always send the claims in to the medical insurance, because it was due to an ACCIDENT and therefore is now medically necessary to bring that person back to their healthy state.

When sending a medical claim you have to stop thinking from a dental standpoint and start thinking from a medical one. For instance: You have a diabetic patient with periodontal disease. You do not want to think only in terms of that they might lose their teeth; instead, think of the infection they have and the fact that it is spreading through their body until we get the periodontal disease under control. The spreading infection needs to be treated for the overall health of the patient, stopping the tooth loss is just an added benefit.

Verification of Eligibility & Benefits Form

Today's Date:_____ Patient Name: _____
Date of Birth: _____ SSN: _____
Primary Insurance: _____ Phone Number: ____
Plan Identification Number: _____ Group ____

Insured's Name: _____ Insured's SS# _____ Is This Plan a: PPO In Network   PPO Out of Network Commercial/Indemnity – Addres for Claim Submission Ins Rep: _____ Direct Line: _____ Employee Initials: _____

Breaking Down the Claim Form

You are going to need to get some medical claim forms if you are going to submit claims to medical insurance. The form you are going to need is the CMS 1500. These forms are inexpensive and you can get them from the AMA. You will have to use the RED form; the insurance companies will not accept anything else. Your practice management system may allow you to send the claims electronically. This would be the best option if it can be accomplished.

Here is a line by line breakdown to assist you in filing out the claim form. Something important to remember on these claims is not to use punctuation. The computers will throw the claims with punctuation out and you want them to be read by the computer. Use spaces to separate whenever possible.

Lines 1-11   Pretty self-explanatory and are filled out the same way they would be on a dental insurance claim form.

Line 7   If Line 4 is the patient, then this line does not need to be repeated.

Line 10   If this line is answered Yes on any of them, then the Worker's Compensation, Motor Vehicle Accident Insurance, or Other Insurance will need to be filed first

Line 11   Make sure to mark (d) No if they do not have any other insurance

Line 12&13   Self-explanatory as well, but we want to make sure you know that you <u>can</u> use the Signature on File here also.

Line 14   This is the date of the current illness; it is the <u>diagnosis</u> date. You will use this date on every claim form pertaining to this illness

Line 15 This line is not usually filled in because it is just giving the insurance company a reason to deny the claim as pre-existing

Line 16 Only used if it is a Workman's Compensation claim

Line 17 Referring doctor -If using this line, make sure a report is sent back to the referring doctor and fill in line (b) which is the referring doctor's NPI#

Line 18 Probably not needed, but if the patient was hospitalized for these services then this is where you would put that date

Line 19 This line is for a mini note (ie: x-rays attached, narrative attached, etc.; can even say SOAP attached)

Line 20 Outside lab—not going to use this too often

Line 21 This is where you are going to put your Diagnosis codes (the ICD-10 codes); this is WHY the patient is here today
- You want to be **very specific** here
- Start with the most horrific problem and then go down from there
- Your first listed diagnostic code is what you are going to SOLVE (ie: inflammation)

- The very last diagnostic code is the contributing factor to the problem (ie: heart disease)
- You only need to have 1 code listed, but can have up to 4
- Use the codes with **5 numbers** (these are the most specific)
-

Line 22   If Medicaid was already submitted, and denied you will enter the denial # from the refusal here; this is not used very often, generally you will just call Medicaid and then fill it out online

Line 23   If you have a precertification or preauthorization #, enter that here

Line 24   The first item listed here should be the most **expensive** of the procedures for that date range. The medical insurance generally pays the most on the first item, and then it goes down from there.

A) Your dates From and To are probably going to generally be the same dates

B) Place of Service is generally going to be #11-office, unless you happen to do hospital visits

C) You just enter Y or N here on whether this is an emergency

D) This is where the CPT or HCPCS codes will go along with any Modifiers that may be needed (this is all covered later in this text)

E) Used to specify which diagnosis code applies - must always be filled in with at least one - if only one Dx is entered in box 21 then 1 will be the number entered. If there's more than one Dx used then 1,2 would be entered.
F) Charge
G) Units (This is how many you are doing). For example <u>1</u> full mouth set of x-rays or exam, <u>2</u> Implants, etc.
H) Rarely Used
I) Rarely Used
J) This is where the doctor's individual NPI goes

Line 25   Federal Tax ID #

Line 26   This is actually the CLAIM #; It does not an Account #; This is usually generated from your software; You can just give it a number for your own use

Line 27   Mark YES

Line 28   Total of all charges listed

Line 29   This is used if this claim is a secondary for what the primary paid; don't forget to change the Balance Due also.

Line 30   Total of all charges listed

Line 31   Dentist's signature and date

Line 32	Office Information (Including address & Corp NPI#)
Line 33	Provider Info (Including address & Corp NPI#)

Your claim form is complete.

CPT Codes

You now know how to complete a medical claim form. Now what are the codes that you are going to need to use when sending these claims? When submitting dental claims, we use the CDT codes (or Current Dental Terminology) to tell the insurance company what services we completed. The same is true with sending medical claims. There are a few differences and you are going to have to make yourself very familiar with these.

The first is you will not be using CDT codes; you will use CPT codes (or Current Procedural Terminology). This is a system developed by the American Medical Association for standardizing the terminology and coding used to describe medical services and procedures, just like the CDT codes are for dental. To get a comprehensive listing of these you can buy the companion to the current CDT book. This book has the CDT code listed with a corresponding CPT code that you can use when submitting to medical. You can purchase this book from the ADA. We recommend purchasing this book; it is well worth the investment. The CDT codes are updated yearly, so it would be prudent to get the latest issue every year.

You can also get a list of these codes from the AMA, but beware, their list is very comprehensive and includes ALL medical codes, including resetting a broken arm, blood testing, etc. The CDT Companion is much easier to use in that regard.

ICD-10 Codes

The next type of coding to be used is the ICD-10 System. This is the International Classification of Diseases. They are the Diagnostic codes that will be used to establish the medical necessity of the CPT code. You will use these to tell the insurance what is "wrong" with the patient. Again you are going to want to limit the ICD-10 codes you are looking at because there are about 14,000 and we will use at most 100.

These codes are from 3 to 5 digits. It is important to know that the 5 digit codes are the most comprehensive so they are the best ones to use.

Modifiers

You will want to use a modifier if you need to add more information about the procedure, want to eliminate the appearance of duplicate billing or if you want to bundle procedures together.

Modifiers can help with case acceptance. They are used when the circumstances of the code have changed, but not the definition. For instance, if the procedure was bilateral, there is a modifier for that, or if the procedure was done twice on the same day you can use a modifier to explain that.

When sending medical claims, one of the most important parts of the claim is the narrative that goes along with it. Using S.O.A.P. Documentation will help you accomplish exactly what the insurance company is looking for in their report. It is a simple way of reporting to make sure you have every part that you need.

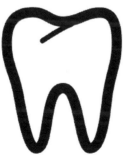

S.O.A.P. DOCUMENTATION:

S=Subjective (What is the patient's chief complaint?)

O=Objective (What did you see? What tools did you use? (ie: xrays, perio probing, etc)

A=Assessment (What is your diagnosis? Make this short and sweet-use your ICD-10 codes)

P=Plan (What treatment will be provided?)—This is your treatment plan. You want to tell them **everything** that you are going to do for this problem. It is OK if you do not do it all, but if you do not tell them everything then they will not pay for what you do not have on the treatment plan (not just THIS appointment—the whole treatment plan).

*You will want to send a copy of this to the medical insurance with the claim. If the procedures are being completed over a series of appointments, you will want to send the SOAP in with the first claim.

This way the insurance company will know the treatment that is going to be provided throughout with your treatment plan.

You can then copy this SOAP and send it with each of the subsequent claims.

Another thing to be mindful of when you are sending medical claims is that this is just coming to the forefront. A dentist sending claims in to a medical insurance is not something they are used to seeing. Therefore, you are going to have to be persistent with the insurance companies. They are probably going to initially deny your claims.

You HAVE to appeal them. Studies have shown that about 50% of offices will not appeal a denied claim.

Send the appeal! Get your patient the benefits they deserve!

What are you going to do if your claim gets denied? Well, you are definitely not going to give up. Sending an appeal letter is fairly easy once you learn how to do it. Here are some important points to include in the appeal letter so that the insurance will take a look at it and review the claim.

First, your RE: should include:
- Patient Name
- Patient ID #
- Claim #
- Date of Service

You will then tell them you are disputing their denial of the claim:
- The insurance plan's reason for denial
- Explain the patient's complaints

- Show that your findings are medically based
- List the tests and x-rays performed, the conclusion of the results and add the ICD codes for each one
- The patient's treatment plan
- Tell what improvement in health status will result or has resulted from the procedure(s), (e.g. improved function, reduced inflammation, etc.)

To end the letter, thank them and tell them that you anticipate payment as soon as possible.

And off it goes...

Your patients will appreciate your "going to battle" with the insurance company on their behalf; after all you are saving them money.

Chapter 4 Recap

If your office decides to send claims to medical insurance you will be providing your patients with a great service. You need to be familiar with the services that are covered under medical benefits:

- Trauma Related Procedures
- Appliances
- Screenings
- Oral Systemic Health procedures

Sending claims to medical insurance you have to:

- Determine if the procedure is medically necessary
- Verify eligibility
- Understand the medical claim form
- Utilize CPT, ICD-10 and Modifier codes used with medical insurance
- Use SOAP documentation
- Be prepared for denials and the need to send an appeal letter

Understand and utilize the patient's medical insurance. If there is a possible benefit, you are not only helping the patient, you are helping your practice as well.

Chapter Five

HANDLING HYGIENE

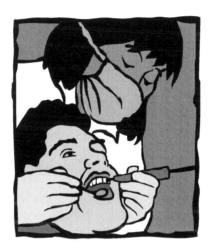

A successful hygiene program is essential to your dream practice. It is the foundation on which your practice has to be built otherwise it cannot survive. Practice's worry all the time about how many new patients are coming in to the practice...if we do not have a good recall system in place, there will be just as many, if not more, walking out the back door. That is not a system that is going to work if we want to prosper.

The question is: How do we create a **solid recall system?**

First, we need to start with the practice's philosophy regarding the hygiene department. This should start with a meeting with the entire team. Of course, the overall philosophy will come from the doctor and most often the hygienists, but the whole team should be involved in the process so everyone knows the practice's philosophy and treatment of preventative procedures and periodontal disease.

After we have decided on a philosophy for the hygiene department, we now need to adopt a process of how we are going to keep up with those patients. This is our **RECALL SYSTEM**.

THE RECALL SYSTEM

One of the many concerns in a dental practice today is having an effective recall system. Every office has a different recall system and all practice management software handles recall a bit differently. Any recall system is only as good as the person responsible for its accomplishments and the success of the practice. That person must monitor it constantly and consistently for the system to be effective.

Over the past few years many offices have started to avoid using the term 'recall'. It is perceived by some to have a negative connotation to the routine professional cleaning. Some feel that the term 'recall' decreases the importance of the procedure. If the patient thinks that it is just a cleaning, the visit will lose its value as a preventive measure to reduce tooth decay and periodontal disease.

With that in mind, many hygienists have begun to use alternative terms such as:

- Continuing care
- Preventive care
- Recare

- Professional cleaning

Remember that words you use, register with your patients and by using terms of value, patients will be more likely to schedule an appointment and will not be as apt to cancel or fail to show.

In addition, they also more accurately describe what procedures are being performed by the hygienist and straightforward verbal skills will help to make a continuing care system successful. For the purpose of this chapter, we will be referring to scheduling a patient for their routine hygiene appointment as recall.

The most important thing is for your practice management software to include a recall system that your office can understand and use. If the software is too complicated to use, get a new software system or offer training for your staff to get them up to speed.

One common recall system allows you to automatically create a new appointment at the time of patient checkout. The software will place the new appointment six months out or at whatever time interval your patient's care is set. You can modify this recall appointment's time and date to accommodate the patient's schedule.

Having something as simple as your patient coming in one day too soon for insurance purposes may be seen by some as incompetence on your part along with an added expense for your patient or undesirable write-offs for the office.

PRE-APPOINTING THE HYGIENE APPOINTMENT

An active pre-appointing system is far more productive and creates a superior recall system that will improve the efficiency of any dental office. Practices that are committed to pre-appointing in the correct manner will swear by the benefits. This is the best option to take whenever possible.

Good organization and outstanding verbal skills will help patients respond favorably to this system. If the patient often declines, it is usually because the hygienist asked a closed ended question: "Would you like to schedule your next visit?" A closed ended question requires only a yes or no answer. Most often, the response to this kind of question is, "I don't know my schedule that far in advance, go ahead and send me a postcard and I'll call you."

To maintain control of the conversation and a positive response, the hygienist should inform the patient what is going to be done.

"Mrs. Smith, your next professional cleaning appointment will be in May. I can see you on Tuesday the 1st or Wednesday the 2nd. Which of these would be the most convenient for you?"

You will have the occasional patient who does object to pre-appointing. In this case, the hygienist might say:

"I understand, Mrs. Smith. We will mail a postcard/send an email to you three to four weeks prior to your scheduled appointment with the day, date, and time of your appointment. Should you find any problem, I will be glad to re-schedule your appointment at that time."

Create an image for the patient that conveys that you are doing them a favor. This requires advanced verbal skills, a pleasant personality, and a genuine desire to make everyone happy.

Postcards or emails should be sent out three to four weeks ahead of the scheduled appointments. This reminder gives patients sufficient time to reschedule their appointments if necessary and gives the appointment coordinator sufficient time to repair any openings in the schedule.

When dismissing the patient at the completion of the treatment, whether with the hygienist or the dentist, create a perception of value and importance in the mind of the patient by saying, for example, "Take care, Mrs. Smith, I'll see you at your continuing care appointment in May. I want to be sure that the tissue around the crown that I seated today remains healthy." Every patient should be released with the reminder that there is another appointment, even if it is 6 months from now.

What happens to those patients that do not pre-appoint? In 6 months, someone gets the daunting task of running the report and calling these patients and/or sending correspondence to let them know they are due to come see you. This is one of the most hated jobs because there is little reward for so much work. Before a call can be made, research has to be completed- when was the last hygiene appointment, what does the insurance allow, what x-rays are needed, how long is the appointment to be scheduled for and is there a balance? – Then all the phone numbers are called and messages left at each number.

Typically only 1 in 20 calls are 'hits'. An effective recall system needs to personally get in touch with your patients at the right time of day, which is not necessarily the best time of day for your patients. Statistics prove that it is easier to get a hold of patients in the evening times, between the hours of 5 and 8 pm. Do you see why it is so much more efficient to pre-appoint?

Most treatment is scheduled following a recall appointment. This is why it is crucial to make sure that your recall system is rock solid.

FAILURES AND NO SHOWS

Appointment failures result in the loss of man-hours for providers and should be kept to a minimum. There is no single best way to handle appointment failures. You can help eliminate them by impressing upon patients the importance of keeping them with correct and professional verbiage. If time permits, you could contact patients by telephone before their appointments to remind them of the date and time. In many cases, patients love the option of receiving text messages one day or even one hour before their appointment.

There are offices that threaten with a cancellation fee, which seems to lead to an accounting nightmare and mad patients. What about those patients that call after hours to leave the bad news that they

will not make their appointment? Some offices have a pre-recorded message that the phone doesn't accept messages, and follow with, "if you need to break or reschedule an appointment for tomorrow, please call the doctor at ***-***-****". That could be a serious deterrent.

Regardless of your methods you will have broken appointments &/or cancellations. When this happens, you should utilize the broken, unscheduled or ASAP lists. It may be possible to fill the appointment time with a patient waiting for treatment.

WRITTEN PROTOCOLS

It is important to have protocols written out in your practice so everyone knows what

is expected as well as knowing exactly what to do as situations arise. We like to see offices have a protocol for their recall system as we have discussed, but also for x-rays and periodontal treatment.

X-RAY PROTOCOL

Having an x-ray protocol in your practice is very helpful. It keeps everyone on the same page and avoids the continuous questions of "Do you want me to get an x-ray?" When developing your protocol, start thinking about every time an x-ray is taken. How often do you take a full mouth series? 4 bitewings? Vertical bitewings? Panorex? When is a PAX necessary? Of course the doctor always has to prescribe the x-rays for a patient, but wouldn't it be simpler if we already knew what the protocol was for a given situation?

PERIO PROTOCOL

Diagnostic procedures should be standardized so that all clinicians are following the same protocol. The doctor and the team should sit down and develop the periodontal protocol for the office. This should be happening in that initial team meeting we discussed at the beginning of the chapter.

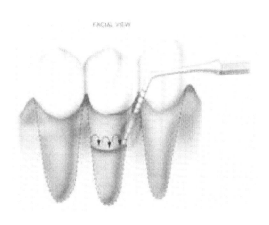

For instance, how often does the doctor want a full 6 point probing performed? When is scaling and ro_ot planning recommended to the patient? How often are we recalling patients? 6 months? 4 months? 3 months? Why? And so on.

A good way to start this process would be to decide what your practice's definition of a healthy mouth is. You could say a healthy mouth is one free of bleeding, 3mm perio readings or less, no cavities, no decay, etc. This is a good subject for a team meeting and should be developed so that everyone knows what to look for to determine if the patient's mouth is in its healthiest state.

Here are a few facts that should be understood when developing your standard of care:

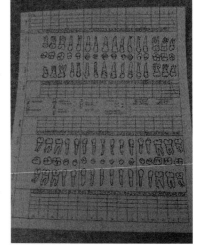

1. General dentists are only devoting about 5% of their time to periodontal treatments.
2. There is a significant amount of dental disease

occurring in our population that is NOT being diagnosed or treated.

3. A hygienist can be held liable if signs and symptoms of periodontal disease are not addressed and documented.

4. In most states, it is illegal for the dental hygienist to "diagnose", although the hygienist as the clinician most often is assessing the patient for periodontal disease.

5. Warning signs of periodontal disease include:
   ❖ Gums that bleed easily
   ❖ Red, swollen, tender gums
   ❖ Gums that have pulled away from your teeth
   ❖ Persistent bad breath or bad taste
   ❖ Pus between the teeth and gums
   ❖ Permanent teeth that are loose or separating
   ❖ Changes in the way the teeth fit together when biting
   ❖ Change in the fit of partial dentures

6. The Co-Examination means that the patient understands how the diagnosis was determined. This

is done by showing the patient a normal sulcus and a pocket. The objective is for the patient to see and understand their own disease as evidenced by pockets, bleeding, and other abnormalities. Explaining the "rules" of the exam before starting so that your captive audience will be able to access the disease with you. "I will be calling out numbers- 1,2,3,etc.; healthy numbers are 1-3; areas of periodontal disease begin with pocket depths of 4,5,6, etc." Call out the numbers so that the patient is allowed to co-diagnose the disease with you. You have a "captive audience" in your lap. Use that time to create value for the treatment that you can provide.

7. Good Clinical Records are essential for diagnosis and treatment planning.

8. What Needs To Be Documented? Pocket depths, bleeding points, suppuration, recession, furcation, mobility, bone loss and plaque.

9. The Patient Chart is a legal record

10. Common Mistakes include: Inconsistency, Omitting obvious information, Vague Language, Improper Abbreviations (WNL), Spelling Errors

11. All dental care providers in the office should be using this same format consistently.

12. Record of Treatment – BP & Pulse; Record treatment rendered including any meds with dosage, Documentation of intra-extra oral exam, Note if premed was taken, Record a Periodontal Diagnosis at Each Hygiene Appointment, Assessment of patient's oral hygiene care, Planned Periodontal Therapy

13. Remember…… Documentation is proof that proper care was rendered to your patient!

14. What to do if the patient refuses treatment? Give patient the declination; have them sign it, **before** you perform a "Coronal Polishing". (See Figure 4.1)

15. Dental Benefits- The treatment protocol for the patient should never be dictated by their benefit carrier, yet once the ideal treatment protocol is established for the patient, make every effort possible to maximize the patient's benefits.

Most treatment is scheduled following a recall appointment. This is why it is crucial to make sure that your recall system is rock solid.

Figure 4.1

Informed Refusal Periodontal Treatment

I am aware of the periodontal disease (gum disease) and infection present in my mouth. I hereby release from liability Dr. _____ and his or her associates, hygienists, employees, and agents from any injury I may currently, or in the future, suffer as a result of my refusal to proceed with periodontal treatment or referral as recommended.

The recommended treatment plan, alternative treatments, and the benefits and risks involved have been fully explained to me to my satisfaction and I have had all of my questions answered.

Inadequate or non-treatment may result in the progression of my periodontal disease with the possible loss of gum tissue, bone and teeth. My periodontal disease may have adverse effects on my total body health. I fully understand these consequences and am willing to assume all of the risks involved.

I have carefully read the above, and understand this refusal for treatment.

Patient Signature _____ Date _____

Witness_____

Chapter Five Recap

Recall, or continuing care, is the one of the most important systems that you can organize in your practice. The key to a successful continuing care program is to make sure that it is a routine task, just as putting in payments or making a deposit. It is too easy for your patients to fall through the cracks. Most patients do not keep up with their continuing care due date.

Key ways to maintain a healthy Recall system:

- Pre-appointing the hygiene appt – it is far more productive to pre-appoint than to try to find the patient 6 months later
- Failures and No-shows – professional verbiage and persistent confirmation methods will help reduce these schedule killers

- Written Perio protocol - Diagnostic procedures should be standardized so that all clinicians are following the same protocol.

REACTIVATION CAMPAIGN
By Denise Ciardello

Let me take you back in time ... Remember when you first opened your doors? Possibly you were right out of dental school, or heading into an established office as an associate, or maybe you'd moved your practice. How did you get the new patients then? Did you and your team sit around in hopes of new patients walking in the door, money in hand, ready to accept that long-needed treatment? I dare say NOT!

You busted your tail putting out fliers, meeting the neighbors, visiting community schools, going to the Chamber, Rotary, or other area meetings. Every patient that walked in the door was like gold to you and you treated them that way; everyone on your team did as well. You knew each new patient by name, who had referred them, what their fears were, and you catered to those fears. You sent them welcome letters and thank-you notes. All became right in your world.

Now here you sit today, one, 10, or 30 years later, looking around, wishing you had more new patients. Why? Where did they go? Those patients that you had acquired haven't stuck around. So why not? Were they stolen from you – possibly by some other dentist with a new practice that is now treating them like gold, knows them by name, who their children are, and what fears they have? They are sending out welcome letters and thank-you notes. At what point did your practice become so full that it was no longer necessary to know your patients by name and show them appreciation?

It's time for your reactivation campaign to gear up, and the organization of this campaign needs to be methodical and systematic. You have a database full of patients who have not crossed your threshold in years, and chances are they haven't been to another dentist since they last saw you. Find them, call them, and welcome them back. The first step is to get your resources all working in the same direction. Your software contains reports to tell you who these patients are and how to locate them. Depending on the size of your report, your team may need to divvy up the list and tackle it as a team. Each patient has different needs, personalities, and attitudes, so your team will need a standard script for approaching these patients. It's not that they have to say the exact same words but the meanings need to correlate with each other. Goals need to be set to carry out this campaign effectively, and the entire team needs to be onboard with those goals. When implementing a plan of any kind, the critical, most important step is to put it on paper. It seems overly simple, yet those that do it understand its power.

Here are some steps to get you started:
1. **Set goals** – Specific, measurable, and defined: how many calls, letters/postcards are going out each day/week/month.
2. **Actions** – Define the exact steps you must take to get to the goal.
3. **Deadlines** – Realistic, but achievable.
4. **Routine review of results** – Don't leave this step off; this is how you determine the success of your campaign.

5. The methods you take to perform this task largely depend on the size of your report. Phone calls are invaluable when trying to reconnect with patients; however, they may not always be possible. If unable to reach a live person by phone, drop a letter or postcard in the mail. There are many services available that will attempt to reactivate patients in your database using electronic means. It doesn't matter what your process is; it does matter that you begin – **TODAY**!

Roadblocks will arise and, as a team, those should be predefined and dealt with according to your guidelines. For instance, a patient's phone number has been disconnected. Do you:

1 – Delete or inactivate the patient and move on? Or…

2 – Go to whitepages.com and try to find at least a valid address?

Dig through the file; there may be a spouse's number or an emergency number that is usually a parent or close friend. What if a patient can't be reached by phone? Do you drop a letter or postcard in the mail? Do you have e-mails in your patients' files? If not, you should begin gathering those today.

Ten years ago, you would never have dreamed of not acquiring a patient's phone number. E-mail addresses are just as significant, or possibly more so today.
In the morning meeting, when reviewing today's patients, it is just as vital to mention the reactivated patients as it is the new patients. Treat them, as you do all your patients, like gold – call them by name; know who their children are; send them handwritten thank-you notes; show them that you appreciate them. When trying to deal with the state of today's affairs, sometimes it's as simple as looking back to the beginning.

Article published in DentistryIQ 5-26-2010

Chapter Six

TREATMENT PLANNING

What is treatment planning?

It is the process by which a dentist, along with the patient, diagnoses problematic dental areas; this diagnosis could be decay related, periodontal related or occlusion related. These problematic areas are ranked in order of need and together a decision is made concerning how to resolve these areas through treatment methods and resources.

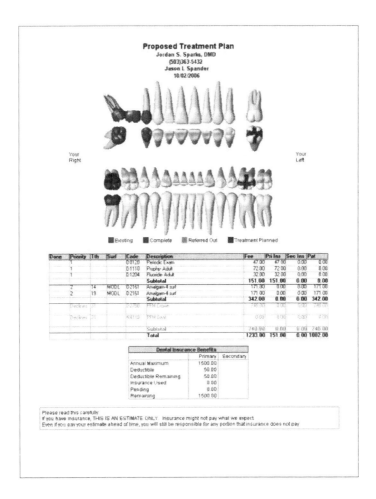

This is an area where your office's standard of a healthy mouth, as discussed in the previous chapter, can be used. Once you have determined what a "healthy mouth" is, you are then able to tell the patient what procedures are needed for their mouth to meet that healthy standard.

For instance, if the patient has any decay they need to have that decay removed and the tooth structure repaired. If they have bleeding, significant bone loss and 5+mm periodontal readings, they need to have scaling and root planning. The nice part of having a "Healthy Smile Standard" written down and understood by the whole team is that everyone then knows what needs to be done for the patients to be healthy.

Another thing to consider when having the meeting about what a healthy mouth is, would be to have the doctor let everyone know his/her philosophy as to when procedures are required. For instance when does the doctor feel a patient needs a crown vs. a filling? When is scaling and root planning diagnosed? Every doctor has his/her own philosophy and this needs to be discussed with the team so everyone knows what to expect.

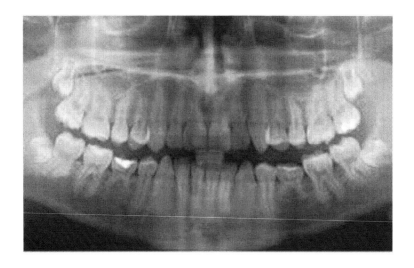

Now that everyone knows what the doctor's philosophy is on when procedures are required, it is then easy for the team to discuss with the patients about the doctor's recommendation. "There is a significant amount of decay on your tooth, and once we clean out the decay there will be very little tooth structure left. Dr. Molar recommends that we place a crown over the tooth. This will strengthen the tooth structure and extend the life of the tooth."

The team does not diagnose a patient's dental needs by any stretch, but they can prepare the patient for when the doctor comes in. For example, if the hygienist has a patient that she sees an area of interest and feels pretty certain that the Dr. will probably recommend a crown on #3, she could pre-frame the patient by telling them:

"Mr. Mouse, it looks like you may need a crown on that tooth on the upper right. We will have Dr. Molar take a look at that when he/she comes in to see you."

By doing this the patient is hearing from both the hygienist AND the doctor that they need a crown on this tooth. It gives more credence to the diagnosis and makes it feel less like the doctor is just trying to "sell" them something.

While still in the operatory, the doctor or team member will explain the procedures recommended to the patient. Details of what the problem is, what options they have to treat it and what could happen if they choose not to delay treatment. This is the most important part of the treatment plan. If the patient does not understand that they have a problem, then they are not going to be compelled to fix it.

"Mr. Mouse, the cavity on tooth number 13 is a 3 surface cavity. If it grows any bigger will turn into a crown, or even worse a root canal. Dr. Molar wants you to come back as soon as possible so we can stop the spread of decay and prevent more work from being needed."

Once you have explained the patient's treatment, it is time to either enter this information in to the computer or type it out for the patient. This information will need to include the following, and then be presented to the patient:

- Office information
- A list of all procedures diagnosed; ranked in priority order
- The cost for the services to be performed, including insurance if necessary
- Expiration dates of quoted fees

- Any disclaimer concerning 3rd party payments; ie, insurance, etc.
- Financial options &/or arrangements
- Signature of patient

Following the treatment plan has been presented to the patient, the clinical team escorts the patient to the business office. The Assistant or Hygienist gives explanation of the treatment plan to the treatment coordinator with any and all, recommendations by the doctor. If the verbiage in the operatory was compelling, the patient will be ready to schedule right away.

It is the job of the treatment coordinator to accomplish that goal. Presenting the financial options are all that is needed and allow the patient to decide what the best course of direction. No treatment should be scheduled without solid financial arrangements, agreed upon by both parties.

Document all arrangements.

Presenting Financial Options: Each office will have different financial policies. A written financial policy is one document that all patients should be presented with and it is strongly advisable to have it signed as well. This document should be kept in the patient's chart. The following is an example of a financial policy for a fee for service dentist.

Dr. Mark Molar
FINANCIAL ARRANGEMENTS AND DENTAL INSURANCE

We are committed to providing you the best possible care available. Our office is not contracted as a provider for **ANY** insurance company due to the limitations they attach to treatment, regardless of the diagnosis. Our commitment is to you, our patient, not to an insurance company.

Your insurance benefits have been negotiated and purchased by your employer, and offered as a benefit to you. The contract is between you, your insurance company and your employer. We are not a party to that contract and do not have any specific information regarding your benefits.

As a courtesy, we will assist you in filing electronic claims to receive the maximum "out-of-network" benefits you are eligible to receive. Because we have no guarantee of payment or a specific payment amount from your insurance company, we ask that all of our patients secure financial arrangements prior to their scheduled appointments.

We offer several options regarding financial arrangements for treatment. Please check the option(s) you have selected so we may process any necessary paperwork prior to your treatment.

- ☐ **Pay by cash or check** in full at the time of treatment and save another 5%.
- ☐ **Pay by major credit card** in full.
- ☐ **12 month 0% financing from Care Credit**

In this option, you finance the entire amount of the treatment plan. We file your insurance claim electronically on the day of treatment and your insurance benefits will be paid directly to you.

With the health of our patients being our highest priority, we would never want finances to be a barrier to your treatment needs. We believe that you will find something here that is just right for you. We are happy to answer any questions you may have. We are here to help you.

Chapter 6 Recap

Treatment planning is a vital to the survival of a dental office. What is your **"Healthy Smile Standard"**? This needs to be discussed and written down so everyone in the practice knows the standard. You can even make a sign and hang it up for everyone to see and be reminded.

You also need to treatment plan your patients to bring their mouth up to the Health Smile Standard. Once you have your treatment plan, now you can to explain to the patient exactly what they need and WHY they need it. The "WHY" is the most important piece of the treatment plan presentation. This is what is going to entice the patient to schedule the appointment for their treatment. Is the tooth going to fall out if they do not have the work done? Will they need a root canal? Dentures? Will they have pain?

The patient has agreed to the treatment, you now need to set up a financial agreement with them. Do not forget this step. Have financial options available for your patients, and have them in writing for the patient to sign and take a copy home with them. Again, do not schedule the treatment unless you have a solid financial arrangement in place. More detail is presented in the next chapter on financial arrangements and collections.

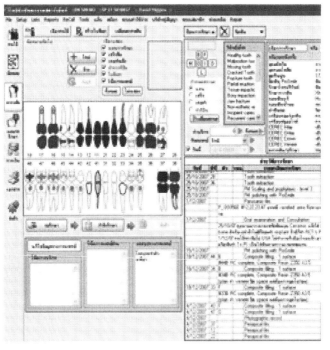

Chapter Seven

$$ All About the Money $$

Most dentists will agree that they got into dentistry because of their belief in patient care. It is their responsibility to fix broken, painful or unattractive teeth. Most dentists take an active interest in their craft and strive to stay up to date with all the latest technological development. Most will tell you that what they do is for the comfort and care of the patient and that it's not about the money.

A wise man once said, "It isn't all about the money, but that is how we keep score in this ball game". The practice can not stay open if the money is not collected – bills, salaries, rent can't get paid if there is no money coming in the door. On the other hand, the quickest way to make a patient angry is when you make them feel as though you are cheating them or stealing their money. If you make all monetary transactions transparent, you will never create enemies. It's not always easy, but it is important to give it your best.

There will always be things that occur beyond your control and more times than not, it involves the lack of payment or a denial from the insurance companies.

Financial Policy

As with any system in a practice, the collection system is only as good as the protocols that are created and those are only effective if utilized appropriately. Basically if you are not collecting money then why are you working? A dental office can produce a million dollars a day but if only $10 is collected, then bills can't be paid, payroll can't be met and the doctor will be frustrated.

> Your dental office needs to have a WRITTEN FINANCIAL POLICY which must be presented to all patients.

Somehow the American public got the idea that it wasn't important to pay the dentist at the time of service. Fortunately, that trend is slowly changing, but oh… so … slowly. It is a duty to your office and all other dental offices to continue changing this trend. There are some of exceptions to this rule, and those will be discussed later in the chapter.

Your dental office needs to have a WRITTEN FINANCIAL POLICY and this policy should be presented to all patients.

Taking it a step further and having the patient sign it is a better idea; be sure to maintain a copy of that signed paper. This policy is the 'rule' by which all financial arrangements are made.

Any questions about how a procedure is to be paid? Refer to the 'rule'. There are three things to remember when setting the financial policy:

1. Make all payment options transparent and stick to it.

2. Offer incentives so patients will pay early.

3. Not one patient is seen before everyone knows what the payment arrangements

Your financial policy will be determined by the dynamics of your office. A fee-for-service office will have fewer options to offer the patients than an office that is in network with several insurance companies.

The following are examples of a written financial policy.

A Fee-for-Service office:

Practice Letterhead
Address
City, State Zip
Phone

OFFICE POLICY AND CONSENT FORM

We are here to serve you in a comfortable and professional atmosphere. Our goal is to provide you with the very best quality of dental care.

INSURANCE AND PAYMENT POLICIES

- FEES FOR SERVICE AT OUR OFFICE WILL BE REQUESTED AT THE TIME OF YOUR VISIT. For treatment involving fees above $500.00, special financial arrangements may be discussed with our office manager.

- For patients with Dental Insurance:
  We will file your claim for you at *no charge*, however, we ask that your deductibles and your estimated portions (20-100%) be paid as services are rendered. Although we gladly file dental insurance claims, any and all account balances are ultimately your responsibility.
  All insurance benefits are assigned to the Doctor, unless services are paid in full the day of treatment.

- Please note for your convenience, we do accept checks and cash as well as VISA, MasterCard, Discover, American Express and Care Credit.

OFFICE POLICIES

- Your appointment time is set-aside especially for you. We ask for courtesy to the Doctor and to other patients that you keep your scheduled appointments. If you must change or miss an appointment, we would appreciate a 48-hour notice. Repeated

cancellations or failures could result in a broken appointment charge or no reappointment.

- We realize that many families are in a state of change. The policy in our office is that the parent who requests treatment for a child is responsible to us for all fees incurred.

- We will be fair in working out special finances with you, but please also be fair to us with your commitments. *A 1.5% finance charge may be assessed monthly on all overdue balances.*

CONSENT:

I have read and understand all the above information. The undersigned hereby authorizes the Doctor to perform those diagnostic and treatment procedures, including local anesthesia and sedation, deemed necessary. If I ever have any change in my health or change in my medication, I will inform the Doctor at the next appointment. For insured patients, my signature below authorizes assignment of insurance benefits to the Doctor and authorizes the release of dental records to my insurance company.

_____   _____

Signature (Patient, Parent or Guardian)   Date

| In-Network |

Practice Letterhead

Financial Arrangements and Patient Communication

We are committed to providing you the best possible care available. Our commitment is to you, our patient, not to an insurance company. Your insurance benefits have been negotiated and purchased by your employer, and offered as a benefit to you. The contract is between you, your insurance company and your employer. We are not a party to that contract and do not have any specific information regarding your benefits.

We will assist you in filing electronic claims to receive the maximum benefits you are eligible to receive. We ask that all of our patients secure financial arrangements prior to their scheduled appointments, in the event that your insurance company fails to pay or the policy is terminated.

We offer several options regarding financial arrangements for treatment. Please check the option(s) you have selected so we may process any necessary paperwork prior to your treatment.

- ☐ **Pay by cash or check** in full at the time of treatment and save another 5%.
- ☐ **Pay by major credit card** in full.
- ☐ **12 month 0% financing from Third party financing (ie., Care Credit)***

*In this option, you finance the entire amount of the treatment plan. We file your insurance claim electronically on the day of treatment and your insurance benefits will be paid directly to you.

There are times when we will need to contact you concerning information that is specific to you, your treatment and your dental needs. Information that is requested to be sent to you by our office via email will be sent in standard email format. We do not have encrypted services available for such communication. We may have the need to use the telephone for confirmation of appointments, or verification of health/dental needs. We will remain mindful all HIPAA laws concerning release of information in these instances.

We understand that things come up that prevent you from keeping your appointment. We ask that you give our office a 24 hour notice to cancel or change your appointment. Failure to notify us within 24 hours may result in a $50 cancellation fee.

With the health of our patients being our highest priority, we would never want finances to be a barrier to your treatment needs. We believe that you will find something here that is just right for you. We are happy to answer any questions you may have. We are here to help you.

_____
Signature of Patient/Guardian

Why do some business owners seldom, if ever, voice complaints about past-due balances, while others spend significant time on this problem?

The answer begins long before a statement is sent. One of the most valuable changes you can make in your collections management is to define payment expectations with your patients in advance of services performed. You can also enter into a formal agreement that includes a commitment to the payment, and then writing out the all the terms.

> Have that Financial conversation.
>
> Formalize the agreement.
>
> Define the terms.
>
> Review it verbally.

- ♦ You have to have that financial conversation - every time. Never hesitate to discuss money with your patients. This normally takes place presenting the treatment plan. Explain in a clear and concise language exactly what you will do for the patient in terms they understand. Quote the full investment and if they have no further questions they can be handed off to your financial coordinator.

- ♦ Your clear communication during this meeting is essential because it establishes important financial policies with the patient. Formalize an agreement. The boundaries discussed at the initial meeting should then be documented in writing. In a financial agreement, you should list the specific services to be performed and the estimated cost of the services or work. This agreement should state how much your patient will owe for work performed or services rendered.

- ♦ The agreement should also specify the terms of payment, including the payment you expect in advance of services. Many professionals that are securing large blocks of appointment times for their patients chose to receive a down payment upon scheduling or at least a few days in advance of their appointment. This allows for a few days of recovery time for your staff should the patient not be financially able to move forward with their treatment.

◆ Review verbally. Take the time to review the agreement with your patient before signing. This will enable you to reinforce the financial obligation that the agreement specifies. You can also use this verbal review time to inform your patient about the value of your work. Confirm that they are making the right choice to proceed with care. As the financial coordinator, you need to establish rapport, and be viewed as an advocate for the patient. There should be no question at the end of your meeting about what the treatment plan is and how much it will cost.

> ➢ There is no greater show of respect than to be clear, up-front, and honest with your clients about money.
>
> ➢ 87% of all malpractice suits involve patients who owe money.
>
> ➢ 50% of all marriages end in divorce. 80% of divorced couples site finances as one of the primary causes of divorce. Clients will divorce you over money too.

Policy / System for creating Written Financial Agreements

What / Why

Written financial agreements ensure that are no misunderstandings about money with patients. It is important to that the patient have a comfortable and clear structure when it comes to helping them make good financial choices for their treatment.

Who

The Dr. is responsible for explaining treatment and explaining the reason that the procedures are needed. Additionally, the Dr. will provide any 'options' for alternative treatment. This assists with having the case sold before the treatment coordinator is introduced to the patient.

The treatment coordinator is responsible for presenting all financial arrangements and filing out all necessary paperwork.

Where

All financial discussions are discussed in the consultation room. If there is not a consult room available, the discussions should be held in most private area of the office.

When

Financial arrangements are done on ALL patients who do not expect to pay 100% at time of service. This also applies to insurance patients.

How

The consult room is set up with a calculator, bottle of water, calendar and any supporting information is up on the computer screen but minimized.

The Office Manager hands the patient a computerized Treatment plan that outlines the treatment and the patient's investment.

The Office Manager builds rapport with the patient by checking in to see if they have questions concerning the treatment plan.

The Office Manager reconfirms the investment and remains silent after saying:

"Mr. Patient your investment is $2000.00, how would you like to take care of that."

If the patient doesn't have questions relative to

treatment but the patient does require payment assistance the following will be offered in this order.

Option #1 > Cash/Check in full.

Option #2 > **Personal Credit Card (Visa, M/C, Etc)** –
r

Option #3 > **Third Party Financing** - Lending Club, Citi or CareCredit

Option #4 > **In-office financing as defined by financial policy.**

Payments should not be coordinated with appointments. Together with the patient, you will determine what the payment dates will be. Essentially they have ninety days to get their balance to zero so it is the patients responsibility to select the payment options that work into their budget.

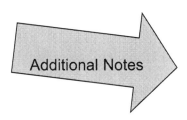
Additional Notes

1. If the treatment coordinator confirms that the patient needs payment assistance and they agree to in house financing the treatment coordinator will run a credit check on the client. If the patient's score is within the parameters of what the office will accept, she would complete the financial agreement document. This document has a line for the down payment, and subsequent lines for the due each month.
2. To improve acceptance, throughout the conversation the OM will congratulate the client on their decision. She will also make a point to focus on the "outcome" of the service. Dentistry can be uncomfortable, expansive and very can be very time consuming. To keep the client focused on the long term vision of their decision the OM will make an effort to keep them future focused by saying "Once we have completed this for you… you will enjoy the benefits of…….."
3. If client is unable to agree to any of the options then the OM has been instructed to discuss with Dr. about altering the Tx plan into smaller phases. If this is not possible then the OM will discuss with the patient a pre payment schedule, or she will place the patient on a holding program with a follow up call to take place in a few weeks.

4. A complimentary benefit check will be done prior to the patient's appointment.
5. The financial agreement will be set up based on the total balance not the patient portion. The patient is told of what to expect relative to benefits but the entire fee is written on the FA. The OM is responsible for communicating with the patient once their benefits have processed.
6. All cases that have a lab fee will be told that the lab fee is due on the date of the first visit.
7. All patients who are scheduled to be the only patient in the office that day (full mouth preps etc) are required to pay their down payment three days in advance of their appointment. This ensures that they will show up.
8. Emergency new patients are required to pay the full fee at time of service. Insurance will be filed on their behalf but the check will be sent to them.
9. There are three copies of the written FAs. One copy goes with the patient the second in the patients chart the third in the ticker system to assist with the daily collection process.
10. If a patient's payment is due on the 15th and they don't send in a payment, collection starts on the 16th.
11. No discounts will be given on credit cards.
12. Senior discounts are 5%.
13. Personal friends of the doctors do not receive discounts.
14. Team members are given $2000.00 a year for dental care. Any team member who needs more care for

themselves, and will be making payments are required to have a written FA.
15. Anytime treatment changes the fees will be discussed. Patient must be seated upright in the chair during that conversation.
16. Since we have written FAs we will not be sending out a statement. Remind the patient of this fact so they do not become dependent on us. For larger cases with multiple payment dates using the coupon book is a helpful option.
17. For patients with dual insurance we will accept and file the primary as a courtesy, the second policy is the patient's responsibility. We will assist them with the necessary paperwork but the check will be sent to their home. They are responsible for paying the balance directly to us.
18. If a patient remits a partial payment DO NOT cash it. Legally once cashed it becomes the new payment. See the collection system for the correct verbiage.
19. If a patient is unable to afford their care, have the doctor rearrange the treatment plan into smaller phases if possible. Sell them something!!!

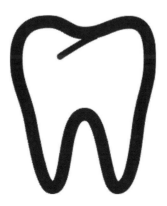

Making a Financial Arrangement

When asking the question, when do you feel it is appropriate to make financial arrangements, the list included:

- Prior to scheduling appointments with associated fees
- When talking with a new patient on the telephone
- Anytime treatment changes – especially during the procedure
- When collecting accounts receivable
- When confirming appointments
- Anytime fees are discussed with a patient
- Anytime a patient will not be paying you 100% at time of service?

What are your criteria? Take a moment to write down the times you will be presenting financial arrangements.

Things to discuss when you write out your financial policy / system

a. Who quoted the fees?

b. What tools will you use and how will it be filed?

c. What services do you want to be paid for in advance of their appointment?

d. What services do you collect 100% of on time of service? (even if the patient has insurance)

e. How do you deal with cases that have a lab fee?

f. What is your system for insurance? How do you file, when do you offer pre auths etc.

g. Can you eliminate or reduce sending out statements?

h. What payment options do you offer?

i. How do you convert existing patients who have a balance over to a written financial arrangement?

j. When there is a change in treatment how will fees be discussed?

k. How do you deal with personal friends of the doctors or with staff members who need treatment and receive special discounts?

l. What needs to be present in the consultation room? Water, calendar calculator etc.

m. How do you deal with Dual Insurance?

n. How long will you honor your fees once they are quoted?

o. What happens when a patient remits only a partial payment?

Financial Options

What options do you want to make available to your patients? The doctor probably has an idea about what should be accepted, but keep in mind  that most dentists are accustomed to allowing patients to pay out their portions.

Always refer to your written financial policy as a guideline.

Insurance Payments

For some offices, payments received from insurance companies make up a huge part of the practice's collections. It is essential to get a handle on these collections, as well as entering your payments for these correctly. All practice management software has specific steps in regards to inputting insurance payments efficiently. Make sure that you are trained in the appropriate processes for effective methods. Please refer to Chapter 3 - *Optimizing Insurance Systems* for complete instructions.

Although insurance does cover some of the patient's balance they are still going to have to pay their portion, or co-pay. Ideally this will be collected at the time of service, but if it is not you are going to need to send them a statement or possibly you may be setting them up with payment arrangements.

By not collecting the amount due at the time of service, you will spend a lot of time and resources chasing that money. Statistics show that 38% of the balance that walks out the door will be spent chasing down that balance. That is a significant amount.

Private Pay

Many patients have insurance, there are still quite a few that do not. They are referred to as "private pay" patients. They do not get the financial assistance from an insurance company. You are probably going to have some financial options available for these patients. This is where you will refer to your written financial policy.

If your office allows patients to pay out their portion, some credit card merchants will allow you to charge the card on a routine basis. There are laws governing maintaining a customer's credit card number so be sure you check into and comply with these before you utilize that process.

3. **Third party financing** – The Lending Club, Care Credit, Wells Fargo, Citi, etc. are a few of the companies that will take on your patients' financial liability. The doctor will pay a fee to this company, then you receive the entire amount charged out immediately. The other company will chase after the money. Again, make sure that you are trained on the proper ways to present, implement and utilize these companies. Most will provide courtesy training. The verbiage you use is helpful when presenting this option to your patients. If there is a problem with this 'loan', it will reflect badly on the office.

The important thing to remember is you are not a bank. Do not put the office in a situation where you have to work too hard to get paid. Any payment arrangements you make with patients need to be written down with the terms of your agreement, have the patient sign the agreement and each of you retain a copy. The doctor typically determines and approves any and all payment arrangements.

Sending Statements

Many offices have scheduled the task of sending statements once a month. For most, it is a huge undertaking that can take the majority of the day. Consider sending statements out on a bi-weekly, weekly or even daily basis. The task is less cumbersome, and you can have money flowing into the office on a more continual basis. Most practice management software systems will allow you to dictate when you want to send statements.

As discussed in the insurance chapter, immediately prepare statements for the patient for any balance remaining after the insurance pays. This prevents you from having to wait another month to receive that payment from the patient.

Things to we recommend are on your statement:
- Your office information, including a phone number
- Credit card option – in the event the patient wants to put this onto their card.
- Online payment options, if you have that service.
- Due date for when the payment should be made; patients will pay whenever they want to anyway but by putting a due date, it gives them an implied notion that there may be a charge for late payment.

- The balance posted clearly on the statement; sounds funny but you'd be surprised how many statements are difficult to read.
- The reason for the balance; have the procedures and all payments listed or jot a note.

Collections

Every office is going to have those patients that make promises and then don't come through with their payments. Then you will need to go through a collection process to get the payment from them. *Make sure you check your collection laws before beginning this process.* The first step in the collection process is of course, sending the statements. If you are not getting a response from your statements, the next step is going to be making a phone call. There are a couple important points to remember when calling patients to collect money.

First, you have to talk to the patient. You cannot leave a message with the person that answers the phone or on the answering machine saying they owe you money. Collection laws dictate when you can call and how often. You can call people at work, but if they ask you not to, then you have to stop.

Don't feel guilty about collecting what you're owed. You didn't fail to keep your word. The debtor did and you have every right to collect. Remember to keep your cool and not let yourself get upset. It's the debtor who should be upset because they haven't held up to their commitment to pay.

Here are a couple examples of conversations when making collection calls:

"Hello, Mr. Smith This is Jackie from Dr. Molar's office. I am calling in regard to your outstanding balance of (amount). We have not received a payment since (date). Is there a problem we need to discuss?"

At this point, give the patient a chance to speak and be very sympathetic to the problem they are having, then continue with the following:

"I am very sorry that you have had this problem, Mr. Smith. However, our accountant was in last week to review these accounts. He will return next week for a report of our conversation. I must give him an amount we can expect to be paid on your account each month and a date of the month on which to expect it."

Here is another useful conversation:

"Hello, Mrs. Jones. This is Carol at Dr. Molar's office. Our accountant has been reviewing our accounts, and he has recommended that yours be turned over to a collection agency. I asked him to please hold off until I could talk with you first."

Then let the patient talk. If the patient senses your caring and willingness to work out payment arrangements, he or she is more likely to make an effort to take care of the account.

If you are unable to get patients on the phone, or are just not having any luck collecting the money that way.

Sending a letter is another option. This is generally the last resort because there is not usually much response to the letters. Here is an example of some wording to be used if writing a letter for a balance that is over 60 days past due:

Figure 7.1

«Salutation»

Your account has a balance of «Balance». Your payment is now overdue. We are assuming that this is the result of an oversight.

However, if your payment is being held up because of a problem, please call so that we can work out a special arrangement together.

> If there is not a problem, we would appreciate it if you could put the payment in the mail today.
>
> If, by chance, your payment has crossed this letter in the mail, please disregard this reminder.
>
> Sincerely,

Or possibly:

Figure 7.2

> «Salutation»
>
> We still have not received your payment and your account balance is «Balance».
>
> Your account is over **60 days** past due. We have extended credit to you beyond a reasonable time period. We feel it is now necessary to receive a response from you.
>
> To keep your account in good standing, and prevent damage to your valuable credit rating, we ask that you do one of the following:
>
> 1) Make payment in full within 5 days.
>
> 2) Contact us immediately to set up definite arrangements for payment of your account balance.
>
> Unless prompt attention is paid to this matter, our accountant insists that we take a more aggressive action.
>
> We are counting on your cooperation.

> Sincerely,

nce the balance is over 90 days past due, a bit harsher wording may be necessary:

Figure 7.3

> «Salutation»
>
> As you know your account is more than **90 days past due**. At this time your account balance is «Balance» and is due. Our records show that we have not received any payments from you since the services were performed.
>
> For one reason or another, you have been unwilling to proceed with payment. Therefore, we have no other choice but to begin a more aggressive action.
>
> Please pay your balance now so that we can avoid any further action—which will be unpleasant for both of us.
>
> Sincerely,

Now, if all of this does not work, unfortunately you are going to have to either send the account to collections or possibly take them to small claims court. Research your options to make sure you choose the correct collection agency. Some of these agencies are very harsh so be sure they are the representatives you want associated with your practice.

Chapter 7 Recap

As with any system in a practice, the collection system is only as good as the protocols that are created and those are only effective if utilized appropriately. Your dental office needs to have a WRITTEN FINANCIAL POLICY and this policy should be presented to all patients. Never feel guilty about collecting what you're owed; you've provided the service and it is the patient's obligation to pay.

There are three things to remember when setting the financial policy:
- Make all payment options transparent and stick to it.
- Offer incentives so patients will pay early.
- Not one patient is seen before everyone knows what the payment arrangements are.

Collecting money is the name of the game, so make it easy on yourself and collect as soon as possible. If there is money still owed after the claim is paid, send a statement out immediately. Remain mindful of the collection laws and always give your patients the dignity and respect they deserve.

Chapter Eight

The Human Side of Business

Check with your state and any governing entities for the laws that pertain to your practice.

Personnel files

Proper maintenance of employee information and observance of the right to privacy in personnel records is necessary to prevent a variety of legal problems. To avoid liability, be sure information in employee's files is accurate and can be validated.

Further, observe the legal requirements governing access to employment data and personal information.

Here are some items to consider regarding employee records:

1. What types of records are to be kept?
2. How will the information be gathered?
3. How will collected information be used?
4. How long must the different types of information be kept?
5. Where are records kept? How are they safeguarded?
6. Who has authorized access to the information?

All personnel files are to be kept in a secure, private area. Only authorized personnel should have access to these files at any time. When records are destroyed, take all reasonable steps possible to ensure unauthorized access to or use of employee's personal data. Information should be shredded or burned,

not tossed into the wastebasket. This applies to electronic data. For example, magnetically swipe a disk before throwing it away to ensure information is not retrievable, if possible shred it.

NECESSARY DOCUMENTS

There are several forms that need to be readily at hand. These include:

1. **Application** (it may be necessary to have one for the different positions within the office). You can create your own or find many versions of applications at the office supply stores.

2. **Job Descriptions** – You do not have to have a description of each individual job an employee does, however, each employee should have written, specific job descriptions that they can refer to often. Upon giving

these descriptions to the employee, a form should be signed by the employee stating that this was received and understood by the employee. A copy of this form should be kept in the employee's personnel file.

3. **W-4** - Federal law requires that this form be filled out and kept on file in the employee's personnel file. (www.irs.gov/w4) Figure 8.2

Form W-4 (2010)

Personal Allowances Worksheet (Keep for your records.)

Form W-4

Employee's Withholding Allowance Certificate

2010

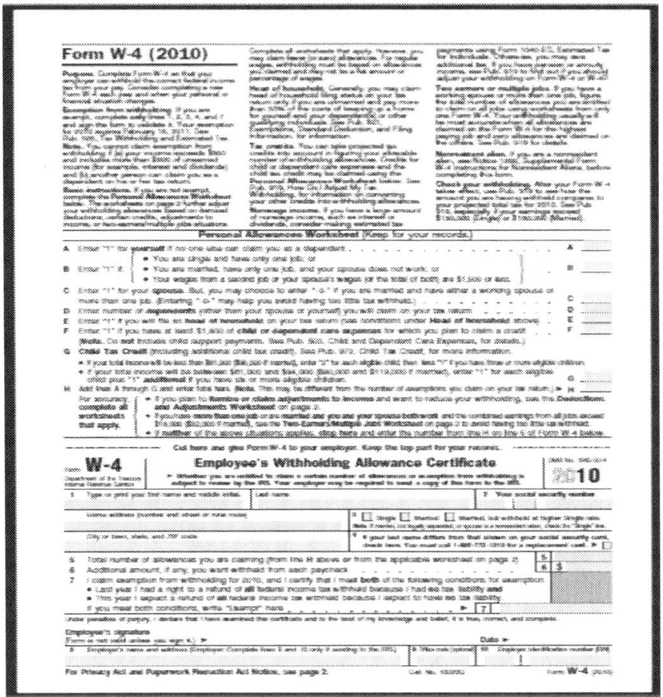

4. **I-9**   Federal law requires that this form be filled out and kept on file in a separate file with all the other employee's I-9 forms; in the event that ICE comes to the practice, all forms may be handed to the agent at one time. (www.irs.gov/I9)

   Please refer to the website listed above. There are 5 pages in total with the form. **You have to ensure that the form is filled out properly and all dates match for accuracy on this form.**

5. **Offer Letter** – Once you decide on a candidate, it is customary to send a letter with the details outlined. An offer letter should try to contain the right mix of friendliness, optimism and disclaimers.

Figure 8.3

OFFER OF EMPLOYMENT LETTER

Dr. Mark Molar, DDS is pleased to offer you the position of _____ for our organization. We are all excited about the potential that you bring to our company. We look forward to you starting with us on _____. At that time, your starting salary will be $_____ per hour. The first 90-days with us are considered a probationary period. Your status during this time is as a new employee with no benefits. If you successfully complete that period of employment, you will be reclassified to regular employee status and may begin participating in our standard employee benefits program.

Since the position calls for the possession of a current and valid State any License or Certification here, please bring a copy with you, so we can document that we are in compliance with regulatory requirements. In accepting our offer of employment, you certify your understanding that your employment will be on an at-will basis. As an at-will employee, you will be free to terminate your employment with the Company at any time, with or without cause or advance notice. Likewise, the Company will have the right to reassign you, to change your compensation, or to terminate your employment at any time, with or without cause or advance notice.

If you have any questions or concerns, please feel free to contact me.

6. **Application Rejection Letter** – it is customary to notify candidates, even if they were not selected for the job. Your letter should be polite, brief, and to the point.

Figure 8.4

APPLICANT REJECTION LETTER

Date

Dear _____

Thank you for your interest in the (POSITION TITLE) position. We enjoyed meeting you.

We were impressed with your credentials; however we have offered the position to a candidate whose background and experience better meet the needs of our practice.

We sincerely wish you the best in your job search.

Sincerely,

7. **Termination Letter**

– When it's time to dismiss an employee, a letter stating what is to be expected is customary. Keep it short and sweet, stating the reason for termination, if you wish, and address any benefits question the employee may have.

Figure 8.5

SAMPLE TERMINATION LETTER

EmployeeName
Address
City, State, Zip Code

Dear Name:

I would like to inform you that your position with the ABC Company will be terminated effective immediately.

Human Resources will provide you with a packet of information (attached) which includes details on a severance package, continuing employee benefits, and your final paycheck.

If I can be of any help during this transition, please let me know.

9. **Attendance/Absence/Vacation Tracking form**

    it is important to document when an employee is out of the office and why; was it approved in advanced?; was it 'excused'? an emergency?
    This can be handled with a simple to excel spreadsheet or with an HR software program.

In addition to all these forms, you should also have a written, up-to-date **Office Policy Handbook.** This document will outline all the policies and benefits the employee can expect during their time with this company. As with all HR forms, *check with your state and any* *governing entities for the laws that pertain to your practice.*

PAYROLL AND TIME CARDS/CLOCK

Although the Fair Labor Standards Act (FLSA) does not require the use of time clocks, they do impose regulations on those employers who do. You need to maintain all payroll records according to your state's laws.

Hiring and Firing

Hiring:
When you hire, make sure that you explain 'at will' employment. You should give an employee manual and written job descriptions to the new hire as soon as possible.

Dismissal:

Even with the best of guidelines, making the decision to discharge an employee is still a very difficult one, calling for the best judgment and objectivity possible. Regardless of how gently the news is broken, the individual is still shocked when discharged. This is not the time for the employer to display anger or to get "even" but rather a time to be concerned about the emotional trauma the dismissal may cause.

 few ideas to keep in mind may include:

1. Do not discuss this with any other employee
2. Try not to coincide the news with a birthday, anniversary, or special event.
3. Take care of business as soon as possible; do not wait until Friday or the end of the day.
4. Make sure the employee understands the reason for the dismissal.
5. Do NOT! Do NOT! Do NOT argue with the employee.
6. Be brief; be delicate; be respectful.

7. Conclude business immediately; ask for keys or any other company belongings.
8. Explain benefits and compensation from that point forward. (Understand your requirements for the final paycheck as per your state)

Chapter 8 Recap

- First and foremost, you need to make sure and check with your state and governing entities for the laws that pertain to your state. This is very important since they differ from state to state.
- Important Facts about Personnel Files:
  - Keep accurate records
  - Files need to be kept secure in a private area
  - Know the necessary documents that need to be kept in the employees file
- Another aspect in human resources is the hiring and firing of employees. Make sure you document everything throughout the hiring and firing processes. This way there are no misunderstandings. Firing someone is never easy so make sure to keep in mind the ideas from the chapter to make sure the process is a little bit smoother.

Chapter Nine

TEAM MEETINGS

Morning meetings or 'huddles' are the most overlooked method of improving daily production and team communication. Too many offices brush off this valuable meeting as something tried but failed in the past, or takes too much time, or worse, can't get everyone (or the doctor) to get to the office in time. First and foremost, all successful offices have daily meetings.

These meetings are not the place for whining or complaining. A precise format can be devised and followed. Many times the doctor or the office manager facilitates the meeting to assure a timely start and finish. The meeting should never last more than 10 to 15 minutes and ALL team members need to be present.

What is covered in the Morning Huddle?

➢ Review the records of all patients scheduled that day to be sure everything is prepared for their visit.

- Hygiene will review for perio exams, doctor exams, x-rays, histories (including updated medical), and unscheduled Treatment plans. Auditing charts for overdue family members helps to keep the recall current.

- The admin team should address any financial concerns, &/or any changes in the schedule (unconfirmed pts, lab cases not in, etc.). Look into the future for any large 'holes' that need to be filled.

- Where to put emergencies for the day?

- Who are the new patients? What are their referral sources?

- Review daily numbers; are we on goal for today? How was yesterday? What does tomorrow look like?

- End the meeting on a positive note – some offices read scripture; some give a thought for the day and others read an appropriate quote. At the very least, a thank you to everyone on the team for a job well done.

See the sample of a checklist in Figure 9.1

MORNING HUDDLES

ADMINISTRATIVE

The following areas are to be reviewed for the next day's schedule.

Check messages (prior to meeting) & make corrections on daily schedule

Note emergency calls that have come in over night

Note unscheduled treatment time available

Report any unconfirmed appointments

Note the number of New Patients scheduled for today and referral sources

MTD Production:
MTD Goal:
MTD Collections:

How many new patients MTD

Discuss patient concerns (Example: Ms. Smith has another appointment and needs to be out on time)

ASSISTANTS

The following areas are to be reviewed for the next day's schedule.

Does the schedule match the treatment plan?

Enough time scheduled for the procedure?

Any unusual materials needed?

Assistant or doctor performing procedure?

Review Medical History/ Updates needed?

Note any allergy precautions

Are pre-meds required?

Lab cases accounted for?

Patient due for recall? Family members due for recall?

Unscheduled treatment remaining?

Is there time in the schedule to allow for additional tx?

Personal Patient information noted for staff

Post treatment calls made and recorded?

HYGIENISTS

The following areas are to be reviewed for the next day's schedule.

Review each chart for any pending treatment that has not been completed

Review each chart for any needed radiograph updates

review Medical History/ Any updates needed?

Are pre-meds required?

Note recall dates for family members/ Do they need to schedule?

Which patients need anesthesia?

Note patient referrals

Select patients for Perio Screening

Select patients for ViziLite Screening

Figure 9.1

Team Meetings

Routine team meetings have a valuable purpose in the process in achieving practice objectives. If you look at each meeting on an individual basis, you probably would conclude that this is a waste of time and production; however, each meeting contributes to better understanding in the office and clarifies expectations of each team member. These steps are the small, continuous improvements that will lead the practice to the results needed to meet team goals.

Objectives

Why are you having the meeting? What are you hoping to achieve? The answers to these questions are what will meet your objectives.

A successful meeting doesn't just happen; it needs to be planned.

⇒ To begin, the date and time needs to be announced &/or posted well in advance of the meeting. Name the team members who should be in attendance.

⇒ Next, you need to have an **Agenda**. Post a piece of paper in the break room with AGENDA typed in big, bold letters at the top of the page. Encourage everyone to put ideas on the Agenda. Topics may include settling different systems performed, training on a new system, going over an old system to get everyone on the 'same page', etc. Next to each topic should be a time frame and who is in charge of bringing that topic to the table. (See Sample Agenda – Figure 9.2)

⇒ Throughout the meeting, each person should be **encouraged to participate**. Ask that if a problem is brought to the table, that a solution accompanies it.

The solution they bring doesn't have to be the final solution; we want to encourage everyone to think of ways to better the practice. Always be supportive of feedback.

⇒ Finally, each meeting should end with **ACTION PLANS** and tasks listed along with the person responsible for their completion. Finally, set a date for when the task should be completed. (See Sample Action Plan – Figure 9.3)

⇒ Effective meetings include:
- Strong leadership
- A clearly defined goal
- Motivated team members
- Achievable goals and tasks
- Support and respect of all team members

"Productivity is never an accident. It is always the result of a commitment to excellence, intelligent planning, and focused effort."
Paul J. Meyer

Figure 9.2

AGENDA

Date: _____ Type of meeting: _____

Start Time: _____ End Time: _____

Facilitator: _____ Recorder: _____

Topic: **Estimated time:**   **Initials:**

1 _____ _____ _____
2 _____ _____ _____
3 _____ _____ _____
4 _____ _____ _____
5 _____ _____ _____
6 _____ _____ _____
7 _____ _____ _____

Pre-meeting preparation needed:
_____
_____
_____

Denise Ciardello   www.GTSgurus.com   Janice Janssen

Global Team Solutions
Practice Management Gurus
Solutions that Work

Action Plan

Practice: _____

Date	Team Member	Accountability Item	Action Taken	Follow-up

Notes: _____
_____
_____

Figure 9.3

How to conduct an effective meeting

Who leads the meeting? The Facilitator is not only a participant but also the person who ensures that the meeting has met all the objectives. The job of the facilitator is to create an agenda from the list of topics brought out by team members.

The facilitator needs to:

- Make sure there is enough time for topics listed
- Keep the meetings and discussions on topic – NO sidebar conversations
- Monitor participation – Encourage clash of ideas not personalities
- Give kudos for accomplishments
- Follow up on previous action plans

Consider this: If team meetings are scheduled during the lunch hour, consider eating before the meeting. Food can be a disruption (passing a plate of cookies always gets attention!) and takes the focus away from the meeting. Block out 30 minutes for lunch and one hour for the team meeting; this will give sufficient time for everyone to eat their lunch and give their undivided attention to the meeting.

The Time Keeper

It is often necessary to assign the role of time keeper to a person without any other role except participant. As the topics are discussed during the meeting, the time keeper will inform the facilitator when the allotted amount of time has been met for any given topic. The facilitator, with the approval of the group, may decide to table the discussion until a future meeting or allow additional time. The additional time will be agreed upon and noted in the minutes. If it is decided to table the discussion, the topic will be added to the next agenda immediately.

The Note Taker

It is important that notes are taken during the meeting and made available to anyone who may have been out the day of the meeting. The note taker may be called the Recorder and this person's job is to take clear, concise notes. It is an important role because what is documented becomes the history of the meeting. It is a requirment that HIPAA is discussed and documented with the entire office once a quarter. The note taker role is very important because they are responsible for documenting this every discussion-taking place during the meeting.

A different person at each meeting can share this role with established guidelines for note taking.

Here are some ideas:

1. Write in a "bullet" format, instead of full sentences. This saves time.

2. Use legible handwriting. If preferred, during the meeting, type notes in the computer.

3. Establish a template for note-taking, such as, "topic", "items discussed", and "outcome".

Efficiency is improved with a consistent format.

4. Write notes quoting the speaker, if possible. Ask for clarification when necessary.

5. Copy the notes and put them in the team meeting binder.

Remember that what is documented becomes the history of the meeting.

The Team

The role of any meeting is to act as a 'thought-force' to provide suggestions, solutions and actions for the betterment of the practice. One of the benchmarks of great meetings is total team involvement. Expect and encourage participation.

The result is greater creativity, more ideas generated, potential for better results, and a team that knows that their opinion matters.

The rest of the team has responsibilities as well; these include:

1. Pay attention to all discussions. Avoid side discussions.
2. Offer ideas, support, and solutions.

3. Voice concerns or objections respectfully and with the reason for the concern.

4. Ask for clarification if something is unclear or not understood.

5. Commit to understanding other's points of view—even when it is different from yours or the group's. Don't expect total agreement 100% of the time.

1. Do not take personal or cheap shots at other team members.

2. Bring a solution along with the problem.

3. This is a professional meeting not a gripe-session or time to air dirty laundry.

When the entire team is engaged communication opens up and the creative juices start flowing. It may take some time to get everyone to participate if they are not used to having their voices heard, but give it time and they will speak up.

Numbers to Monitor

It is important to have a portion of the meeting to go over numbers. Here is a partial list of numbers to monitor. These statistics represent a particular time period, e.g. one month, one quarter, or one year.

Doctor Numbers:
1. Total office production (the total production resulting from all producers)
2. Total doctor production.
3. Total doctor workdays.
4. Daily &/or monthly goals, if different from last month.

Hygiene Numbers:
1. Total hygiene department production / Prod for individual hygienists.
2. Total hygiene workdays/ Average hygiene per day production.
3. Number of quads of SRP.
4. Daily &/or monthly goals, if different from last month.

Account Receivables:

1. Total collections/ Collection ratio.
2. Total credit adjustments (courtesy adjustments, bad debt write-offs, etc.).
3. Total amount written off due to participation in reduced fee-for-service programs.
4. Total account receivables.
5. Account aging: current, 30+, 60+, 90+
6. Insurance aging: current, 30+, 60+, 90+

New Patients:

1. Number of new patients.
2. Referral source information.
3. Case acceptance percentage.

Performance Review

No one likes performance reviews. It doesn't matter if you are the owner, the office manager or the employee; it is a daunting task that everyone hates. Think back to when you were a kid and it was time for report cards to come out –  remember that pit in your gut? Performance reviews are the 'report card' for adults.

The idea behind the review is not merely to yell and scream at the employees, nor is it the time to praise them to the highest degree. The idea is to give an honest assessment of the employee's last year of service to the company and to set goals for the coming year.

Typically this review is conducted somewhere near the employee's anniversary date.

Some managers like to walk in the office in the morning and announce to Mary that today is the day for her review. They feel that the element of surprise will favor their side. This is unfortunate for everyone and it will probably be a waste of time. Instead, be prepared and allow the employee to be prepared also.

The performance review process should be streamlined and impactful. It is a time for the manager to agree upon goals and skills with the employee and then deliver constructive feedback on their progress. Since you can't get out of doing an annual performance review, do what you can to make it a useful tool.

To make your performance reviews as productive and painless as possible, consider these 10 suggestions:

1. **Be Prepared**: Know what you are going to say before you are in front of the employee. Give the employee some tools to be prepared as well. A week before the meeting, hand out a form and ask the employee to complete the form and bring to the meeting.

2. **Be positive** – accentuate the good; praise is a form of leadership that is often overlooked. Be professional and upbeat during the review no matter how it's going; do not argue or make personal attacks. Give specific examples of the employee's positive impact.

3. **Be truthful** - Everyone has areas that need a little work; point these out and discuss how together you can solve any shortcomings.

4. **Be a good listener**- this is the time for both sides to talk about what's going on with the business. Remember

that understanding body language is an active part of listening.

5. **Be Consistent** – if you use a form for one employee and you give them a week to prepare for it, do the same for all employees.

6. **Be on topic** – this is not the time for this employee to gripe about all the other employees; job satisfaction should be the most Important factor affecting an employee's attitude, so include issues most important to the employee.

7. **Be in a discussion** – both sides should be sharing not just you. If need be, have open-ended questions to break the ice and get the other side talking.

8. **Be Real** –Take a moment to share some personal time. Talk about goals, both professionally and personally; determine if there is need to help with balancing of the two.

9. **Be Open to Ideas** – this is a great time to ask what direction your employee sees the company going. Some employees are not comfortable or willing to share ideas unless specifically asked.

10. **Be Regular** – Put it on the books and make it a date long before anyone has the chance to complain that they never have had a review.

The conclusion of the meeting should have the employee feeling acknowledged, appreciated, and valued for the past year's performance and motivated to focus on new, bigger and brighter goals for the coming year. These goals are to ensure success of the employee and for the company.

The thing to remember is that the most important asset you have within your company is your people, your team. Henry Ford once said that if you repossessed all of his factories and burned all of his warehouses to the ground, left with only his people, he could rebuild everything that had been lost.

<u>Salary Review</u>

The only thing hated more than performance review is the dreaded salary review. Many times the two are combined. That is up to the discretion of the employer. This review is conducted usually following the probationary period and then yearly at a specified time.

All employees need to feel that they are appreciated and acknowledged. To some that only comes in the form of money, either by choice, because the employer doesn't give out kudos readily, or by preference since money is the most important thing to them.

Here are some suggestions for a productive salary review:

1. **Put it in writing** – what are you going to write down? How about starting with the job description; then move on to all the benefits. Benefits all have a monetary value, so add them up. If you need a form, see appendix 8.5.

2. **Explain overhead vs. production** – although this is often answered with 'that's the cost of owning a business', it is also the way to a raise.

3. **Bonus plans** – if any, are also to be discussed at this meeting.

4. **Discuss benefits** - Are there benefits that you offer that the employee is not taking advantage of? Mention them and explain the value. A 401K is not too enticing for a 24 year old, so a little education would go a long way for that employee.

Ideally you don't want the performance and salary reviews to be at the same time as they cover different areas. One is based on the employee's performance and the other is based on the company's performance. However, keeping the two topics separate often proves to be a challenge.

"The single biggest problem with communication is the illusion that it has taken place."

George Bernard Shaw

Chapter 9 Recap

Every business has meetings and these meetings can either be dreaded and boring or productive and purposeful. The types of meetings in a dental office include:

- **Huddles** – usually held in the mornings; a quick snapshot and discussion about what to expect that day.
- **Team Meetings** – usually held routinely (weekly, monthly, quarterly); purpose is to communicate as a team in the quest to achieve practice objectives.
- **Performance Reviews** – usually held yearly; the purpose is to give an honest assessment of the employee's last year of service to the company and to set goals for the coming year.
- **Salary Reviews** – usually held yearly; although often mingled with the performance review, this is to review the health of the company and the employee participation in the productivity.

The number one "issue" we hear from staff members is the lack of communication. Implementing these different types of meetings will open up the lines of communication, and help your office to run more efficient and productive.

Chapter Ten

Dealing with
CONFLICT IN THE OFFICE

Office Management Guide®

Conflict is common in any environment and it is inevitable in just about every office environment. Can you think about a time when you were in the store and two people started arguing and you were confused as to what started this whole discussion? It seemed like they were arguing over something so simple that wasn't worth really fighting over.

Why do we have conflict? There are several reasons – we are with our coworkers for more time each day and we are with our own families. If you stop to consider that you tend to disagree with people you're closer to than total strangers, and you begin to understand why there is conflict. As humans, we have the ability to think, which gives us opinions and it is those differing opinions, philosophies and goals that cause the conflict.

Conflict is not a bad thing. In fact it truly is a very healthy thing to have in a work place because that's how newer, bigger, better ideas are founded. Conflict can arise anywhere, anytime and about anything. Conflict is only bad when it becomes heated and then it is just a verbal fight. If left unmanaged, it can escalate to degrees that can create a loss of trust, a loss of productivity and in extreme cases can cause the death of a business.

It is impossible to avoid conflict, and it is best to confront conflict as soon as possible. Herein lies the problem. Most of the time people will say "I don't like confrontation". Yet how do you resolve an aggravation or a situation unless you confront it? If we never confronted a problem, then the world will be running rampant with people standing around wringing their hands with frustration. A situation needs to be confronted before you can find resolve.

The first step in resolving conflict is to

understand conflict management strategies. These strategies are usually brought out because of different types of personalities. There is not a wrong or right strategy to use.

The Five Conflict Management Strategies are:

1. **Accommodating**: One party merely gives in to anything the other party wants. The downfall to this method is that the 'yes' party will typically keep score for future ammunition.

2. **Avoiding**: the conflict is delayed or ignored, hoping it will just go away. At times, this may be a favorable approach, but there can be

eventually bigger issues than the initial problem later.

3. **Collaborating**: the problem, issue or roadblock is put out to the group, then a brainstorming sessions occurs to come up with an answer that everyone can live with.

4. **Compromising**: Both sides give a portion of their position in order to establish an acceptable solution. The parties each hold an equivalent level of power – 2 managers, 2 business owners, etc.

5. **Competing**: One wins, one losses. That's it. Typically an owner exerts his/her power to settle the topic.

The main rule that we like to implement is that if Mary comes to you with a complaint about Lisa, you turn Mary around and explain that the discussion needs to be between Mary and Lisa. If you partake in the discussion, even as a 'listener', you are now partaking in gossip. That is a negative energy that does not belong in an office. It is divisive and should never be allowed. As individuals within the office, you shouldn't want that either.

Let's Talk It Out!

By Chris Ciardello

When I am faced with a problem, I like to grab someone and talk it out. This is a great collaborative strategy to problem solving. Everyone has a different personality, and we all see the world in a different light. What  happens when the problem you have is with another person? I often hear "I just need to vent, to get this off my chest." The drawback with handling your problem with another person is that it now becomes gossip. Gossiping is a cancer in any office or social environment. It builds walls and divides teams. A major subject at our last OMG! Office Management Guide® Workshop was conflict resolution.

Every office has conflict, but not every office handles it the same way. This is why it is a subject that we like to bring up in all of our workshops. We all have diverse personalities and communicate in unique ways. These differences in our personalities are what make conflict resolution an uncomfortable and touchy subject.

The first step to successfully deal with conflict is to bring both parties together and have a meeting of the minds. The parties involved in the conflict need to sit down and talk it out. Prior to this meeting taking place, ground rules, need to be explained.

We suggest the following 4 ground rules.

Rule #1 is that each side must listen fully to the other side before responding. There is nothing more frustrating when someone interrupts you, especially when trying to resolve a problem. The first person listens to everything the other person has to say, and then the second person will have their opportunity to explain their side.

Rule #2 is to identify the issues clearly, professionally, and concisely. Unless the issue is identified, a resolution cannot be found. The reason the Betty gave Sally a dirty look when Sally asked Betty a question could be that Betty got a frustrating text from her child saying they forgot their homework. This has nothing to do with Sally yet the frustration was taken out on her, causing some tension. We don't always know what is going on in another person's life, so try not to jump to conclusions.

Rule #3 is that both parties are only allowed to use "I" statements. "I felt ignored at the meeting this morning when I was trying to explain the details about Mrs. Jones." 'You' statements put people on the defensive. "YOU always put the instruments back wrong." "You never take out the trash." When someone starts to get on the defensive they stop hearing everything that is being said. They are focusing on how to defend their integrity. "I" statements diffuse anger and assault. "I get upset when I can't find the instruments I need." "I feel demotivated when the chart is ripped out of my hands." "It hurts my feelings when a harsh tone is used when asking for a favor." When you bring the problem back to how it makes you feel it will bring guards down and a conversation can begin.

The **final** and most important rule is that there are no personal attacks, name-calling or finger pointing. These are a sure fire way to get the other person on the defensive, and there is just no need for petty attacks a professional environment. Having conflict in an office is ok; in fact, it's actually healthy. However, preventing conflict from turning into heated conflict is crucial to avoid division in an office. If a resolution cannot be found with the two parties sitting down and talking it out, then it is time to bring in a mediator. Often times this will be the doctor or the office manager. Whoever it is, they need to remain as neutral as Switzerland. The mediator cannot and should not pick sides, and the same ground rules apply. We all want to work in a happy peaceful environment, so let's talk it out.

Chapter Eleven

INFORMATION SYSTEMS

As you have discovered, the office manager of a dental practice wears many hats. One of these could be the management of the information systems that are in the office. This would include the computer hardware and software, telephone system, fax, and backup of the data in the computers. These can be daunting tasks at times, but when they go down the whole office comes to an abrupt halt. We cannot have that!

"It is only when they go wrong that machines remind you how powerful they are."
Clive James

HARDWARE

What is hardware? Historically it referred to as the nuts and bolts, hammers, screwdrivers and saws used to build something. Now it is best known in the technical world as the outside of the computer, something you can feel.

Hardware in the office also consists of the computers, printers, telephones, scanners and all networking machines. If you are assigned the task of buying or handling the hardware for the practice you need to do your research. With the explosion of computers, there has also been an explosion of hardware techs and some of them specialize in dental offices. Again, do your research, check their quality and know what you are getting for what you are paying.

As with any business, there are some that are not as ethical as others. Talk to other people in your area; your hairdresser, your medical doctor, probably even your mechanic has a computer and they all use someone to help them. Hardware techs' services range

from just repairing to actually selling and setting up a new system or you can buy the computers on your own and have them do the installation. Networking your computers so they all "talk" to each other is very important and not a task that just anyone can do, so make sure that you get expert help.

Another thing to remember in this process is that all software has certain requirements to run the program. It is important that you get the specs for all the software that you need before you start the purchasing process. The software that is chosen is going to need a specific amount of memory, possibly a video card, and storage space.

Now it is time to talk about the peripherals to the computers themselves. What kind of keyboards do you want? Wireless? Wired? Small? Standard? The same goes for the mouse.

Think about where these are going to be, and make (or help the doctor make) these decisions.

- Do you want dual monitors in the operatories?
- Are you trying to go paperless? If so, think about where patients are going to fill out the paperwork.
- Do you want to have a kiosk in the reception area, or do you want some kind of tablet?

Make sure you have a scanner, and preferably one that has a feeder so that you can scan in more than one piece of paper at a time. You also have to consider whether or not you are going to be scanning in x-rays when considering what type of scanner to get.

A scanner with transparency adaptability is needed if you will be copying x-rays. Or...some offices just put the x-rays on a light-box and take a picture. Will you need to have your documents signed electronically? You can either go with a tablet or some type of electronic signature pad. The bottom line is that all of the equipment needs to be able to 'talk' to each other.

SOFTWARE

What is software? It is the application or the programming language that runs your operating system. What type of software are you going to get, or what kind do you already have?

There are as many practice management software out there for the dental office as you can imagine. Some are very basic while others are incredibly complex. The most important thing about the software is that you know how to USE it. Most software companies will give or sell you some training time with the initial purchase. Get training on the ins and outs of the software so that you can use it to the best of its ability.

If you are purchasing new software, write down everything you want out of it and then start your search.

- Schedule appointments
- Treatment plan
- Track balances
- Track outstanding insurance claims

- Sign paperwork (consents, HIPAA, new patient paperwork, medical history updates, etc.)
- Write and sign clinical notes
- Send electronic claims and statements
- Etc.

Make sure it is easy to navigate and that it does everything you need. There are too many to choose from not to have what you need for your practice. You are also going to want to make sure that everything you want will integrate with the software that you choose, like digital x-rays and intraoral cameras.

Again, they all have to be able to 'talk' to each other. Just because they are all software programs doesn't mean they will automatically talk to each other; much in the same way that all humans do not speak English, German or Spanish.

Back up! Back up! Back up!! Backing up your software and x-rays is another very important task that needs to be done on a daily basis. You can have this setup to run overnight so it is not interrupting anything during your workday. Usually you should have a daily, weekly and monthly backup system in place. Often times, someone should take yesterday's backup offsite at the end of the day so that if there is a fire in the office you will have the most current backup.

Another thing to consider is giving a quarterly backup to the practice accountant or lawyer for security purposes. There are also companies that provide off-site back-up systems. They charge by the size of the database.

Do your research. Ask how long until you can retrieve your data and if there is a limit to the number of times this can happen in a certain period. If tragedy strikes and you do not have a backup, what would happen to the practice?

TELEPHONE SYSTEMS

There are several things to consider with your telephone system. First of all, you should have a dedicated line for the fax and/or credit card line. We do not want a call-in line hung up by faxes and credit card payments. You will also want to make sure you have enough lines and people answering them to withstand your call volume. Patients should never get a busy signal; it simply is not good for business.

Another thing to consider with your phone lines is what type of answering service you are going to use. Whether you have an answering machine or use a service that answers your calls, make sure your message is clear and concise. Do not speak too quickly; people have a hard time understanding recordings so make sure you speak slowly and to the point.

Depending on how busy your office is, you may want to consider having a recording while people are on hold. You can have recordings that talk about specials that you are running in the office, holiday messages or information about the doctor. This is a perfect time to tell your patients about services you provide, your history as a practice and your location.

There are telephone systems now that can pull up the patient's information in your practice management system when the call comes in...it is a form of caller ID. This may be something you want to consider as well. Such great technology out there! Do your research and find out what works best for you.

"Bill Gates is a very rich man today... and do you want to know why? The answer is one word: versions."
<u>Dave Barry</u>

Chapter 11 Recap

The systems that run your office are so very important. In some offices, it may be up to you to make sure these systems are up and running in the most efficient manner. Just make sure to do your homework, and know the systems that you are running. When one of these things go down it affects the whole office, so it is very important not to let that happen.

If you are buying new, do your homework. Make sure you understand everything that you are going to need and plan accordingly. Do not hesitate to ask questions to get the product that is tailored to the needs of your practice.

In this world of technology, we need to make sure it is all working correctly, as well as working together. Enjoy the technology at your fingertips, and make the most of it!

The Definition of Chartless
By Christopher Ciardello

Offices seem to get hung up on is the word "paperless". Paperless means to be without paper – that is the obvious definition; however it is virtually impossible to be completely paperless. You will still have to print receipts for patients, create a letter that needs to be mailed, and reports that will need to be printed for monthly meetings. Many times an office will say they want to become a paperless office, when in reality they want to become a chartless office. Chartless means to be without physical charts.

A large, and often most difficult part of becoming a chartless office is being able to accept new patient

paperwork electronically, sign consent forms, update medical history, and sign clinical notes all in the computer. We get comfortable with our physical charts, they are easy to update, correct mistakes, and there is something about physically holding the chart that makes us feel that the information is 100% secure. The truth of the matter is that as long as the correct systems are set in place, patient records are more secure in a digital format.

Heaven forbid, the community suffers from a flood or the office has a fire. In a nature disaster, physical charts, and all the information contained within them, are completely destroyed. When an office begins to use digital charts, it is recommended (even required in some instances) to have an off-site back up. This keeps the records safe and secure so once the water is mopped up, you are ready to open the doors to patients, it's as if you didn't miss a step.

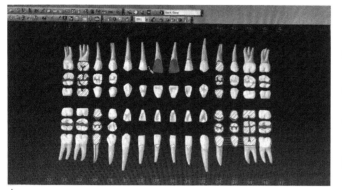

There are certain steps to take to ensure that the transition from a physical chart to a digital one can be very smooth. This is a transition; a project; a journey; not an overnight task. The general rule is that it will take anywhere from 6 months to a year to completely become a chartless office. The length of time it will take to move from physical charts to digital charts depends on how technologically savvy your staff is. A staff that enjoys working with computers will be able to add multiple new steps to the transition, whereas an office that has a staff that is fearful of computers will want to take it one step at a time.

Most of the time when I see an office that is using a combination of a computer program and physical charts, they are using the program for making appointments and keeping track of patient balances. For offices that have no computer program, entering appointments and balances would be the first step. Otherwise, the first step is for the doctor to start signing their clinical notes in the computer. If your software cannot do this basic function, it might be time for you to begin shopping around for a new program.

The next step would be to start charting the patient's existing work and treatment plans into the digital chart. With most software program, anything that has been documented in the patient's ledger is already in the digital chart. You would only need to enter any work the patient had done at another office and their treatment plans. This tends to be the hardest step for an office because these steps are done while the patient is in the chair and the doctor is calling out the work.

Sometimes this will require the doctor to slow down and reevaluate how they call out treatment. With a physical chart it is easier to go tooth by tooth and call out the work that needs to be done. With a digital chart it tends to be easier to find teeth that need to same type of work and call them out together. For example, call out the teeth that need fillings so the assistant can highlight them in the program; then call out the teeth that need crowns, root canals, of scaling and root planning needs to be done, etc. This way the assistant can get everything down correctly.

Once this step has been mastered, we move on to signing consent forms and treatment plans. This is the area that can be tricky because not all software programs have the ability to sign consent forms and treatment plans digitally. I see in many offices the administrative team will have the patient sign a physical copy of the consent form or the treatment plan, then scan it into the document center of their program. They will give the patient the "original copy", or shred it if the patient does not want to keep it.

One downfall to handling the forms in this fashion stems from the fact that the office now has is a "copy" of the

"original document". Depending on which state you reside in, there are some judges who will not allow that in court because it is not the "original document". So if you shredded the document, the court sees it as if it doesn't exist and you are up a creek. The first thing I would do is to find out if your software program can sign these forms in a digital format and how to do it. If it does not, then I would speak to your malpractice insurance company so see what steps they recommend.

Becoming a chartless office is big task to take on, but in the end will be well worth the effort. It will save you time and money in the long run, and increase the value of your practice. Something my grandfather taught me from a young age was to always challenge myself. He encouraged me to embrace technology because it is the way of the future. My challenge to you is to look around your office and see where you can improve it and how you can embrace technology.

Final Thoughts

The role of an office manager is not all-encompassed in this book. There are many aspects to be considered to run a dental practice efficiently. Brand new and seasoned office managers alike will find OMG a great first step in increasing their worth as a leader of a successful practice.

Thank you for purchasing our book. We hope it continues to be a great benefit to you. Please visit our website: **www.GTSgurus.com** often, we strive to update it regularly.

You will also be able to sign up for our newsletter that is filled with great tips and tricks.

"There will come a time when you think everything is finished. That will be the beginning."
Louis L'Amour

OMG! ;-) Glossary

1. **ADA** – American Dental Association
2. **Action plan** – list of things determined in a meeting that need to be done for the office
3. **Admin Team** – workers maintaining the business side of the dental office – also referred as Front Desk
4. **Agenda** – to do list for meetings
5. **AMA** – American Medical Association
6. **Amalgam** – a silver filling material used to restore teeth from decay
7. **Back up** – the act of making an electronic copy of data to refer to in the event of a disaster or accidental deletion
8. **Bicuspids** – the teeth between the canine and molar; they have 2 cusps
9. **Bitewings** – x-ray or radiograph

10. **Body language**- non-verbal communication to determine the level of understanding and the attitude of another
11. **Bonus (Incentive) Plans** – a monetary incentive offered by employers in addition to usual compensation
12. **Budget** – the balance of expenses and revenues
13. **Canine** – the teeth that are right next to the anterior or incisor teeth. Many people refer to them as "eye" teeth.
14. **CDT codes (Current Dental Terminology)** - the terminology and coding used to describe medical services and procedures
15. **Clinical Notes** – the documentation written by the doctor, explaining the procedures completed during a patient's office visit
16. **Clinical Records** -

confidential recording of a patient's dental or medical record
17. **Clinical Team** – Dental Hygienist, Dental Assistant and Dentist
18. **Coronal Polish** – polishing the enamel surfaces of the tooth
19. **Comprehensive Exam** – thorough exam of the entire mouth to determine oral heath
20. **Conflict** – a difference that prevents agreement; a differing of ideas, feelings, etc. between 2 or more parties
21. **Customer service** – policies designed to enhance the level of customer satisfaction
22. **Deductible** - the portion a patient has to pay out-of-pocket before an insurance company will cover their portion
23. **Diagnosis** - determine the causes of symptoms and solutions to issues
24. **Diversity** – encouragement of

tolerance for people of different backgrounds
25. **Effective Date** - the date upon which the insurance policy is considered to take effect
26. **External marketing** – promoting a business outside the walls of the business, such as billboards, radio and newspaper ads
27. **Fee for Service** – patient pays provider directly for services without relying on insurance
28. **Financial Policy** – the method a business describes their alternatives of payment for services rendered
29. **Full Mouth X-rays (FMX)** - complete set of intraoral X-rays taken of a patients' teeth
30. **Furcation involvement** – condition in which bone loss occurs in the bifurcation or trifurcations of teeth; usually due to periodontal disease
31. **Hardware** - all networking

machines, such as computers, printers, telephones, faxes, etc.

32. **Health Maintenance Organization (HMO)** –dental plan the patient has to choose a doctor that is in-network to receive any benefit
33. **Huddle** – when a team gathers together: usually a morning meeting, to strategize and plan the days' events
34. **ICD-10 Codes (International Classification of Diseases)** - diagnostic codes that will be used to establish the medical necessity
35. **Information systems** – all means of communication within a business
36. **Insurance Aging** – tracking of outstanding claims
37. **Internal marketing** – promoting a business with employee and current customers
38. **Job Descriptions** – a list of tasks expected to be performed by an

employee
39. **Letterhead** – formal heading on a sheet of paper; often times imprinted with the company logo
40. **Limited Exam** – emergency – exam of a single tooth or area
41. **Linear booking** – single line booking; putting all the appointments in one line or column
42. **Mandibular Arch** – the lower arch of teeth
43. **Marketing** -- promotion of a business or entity
44. **Maxillary Arch** – the upper arch of teeth
45. **Medicaid** – dental plan through the government
46. **Medical cross-coding** – submitting dental procedures to a medical insurance company
47. **Modifier** - adds more information about the procedure
48. **Molars** – teeth farthest back in the

mouth; will have 4, or sometimes 5 cusps
49. **Occlusal Guard** – splint; a removable dental device used to protect the teeth
50. **Offer Letter** – correspondence to a potential employee, listing the terms by which employment is offered
51. **Office Manager** – position in the office that maintains the flow and organization of an office
52. **Office Policy Handbook** – a list of the company's office guidelines and procedures
53. **Overhead** – the ongoing cost of running a business
54. **PA** – periapical; x-ray taken of single tooth – many times for limited or emergency exams
55. **Pano** - an extraoral x-ray of the entire mouth of the patient
56. **Performance reviews** – the act of evaluating an employees'

accomplishment

57. **Periodic Exam** – the routine exam by the Dr during the prophy appointment
58. **Perio Protocol** – the system used to determine a patient's soft tissue health
59. **Periodontal** – soft tissue or gums in the mouth
60. **Periodontal Exam** – the examination to determine the health of the soft tissue
61. **Periodontal 'Gum' Disease** – plaque build up under the gums causing inflammation and bleeding
62. **Perio Maintenance** – the professional cleaning following periodontal therapy to control gum disease
63. **Periodontal Probing** – a diagnostic tool to determine periodontal disease; a probe is inserted between the tooth and gums to

measure the depth of the pockets
64. **Personnel files** – confidential information about an employee
65. **Practice management software**-- database for a computer system that organizes all patient information
66. **Pre-appointing** – scheduling the next visit
67. **Preauthorization** – the act of filing a claim prior to treatment, to determine what insurance benefit will be allowed
68. **Preferred Provider Organization (PPO)** - insurance plan that allows the patient to see either a provider that has opted-in to their network or not
69. **Primary (Deciduous) Teeth** – a child's first set of teeth; all primary teeth may be lost and replaced with permanent teeth
70. **Profit** – the revenue minus the expenses

71. **Prophy** – (Prophilaxis) professional dental cleaning of teeth
72. **Reactivation** – the act of bringing inactive or previous patients back into the practice
73. **Recall** System - method used to maintain patients in a routine approach
74. **Recession** – the retreating of gingiva exposing the root of the tooth
75. **Referral** – the method in which a customer came to a business
76. **Rejection Letter** – correspondence sent to people who were not chosen for a particular job in which they applied
77. **Restorative services** – the use of certain materials to restore the functionality of a tooth or teeth
78. **Return of Investment (ROI)** – understanding the cost and functionality of a marketing source

79. **Salary review** – determination of an employee's performance and the business' health
80. **Salutation** – the greeting in a written correspondence; Dear ----
81. **Scaling and Root Planning (SRP)** – periodontal therapy to remove bacteria, plaque and calculus from under the gum line
82. **Secondary Insurance** – the patient's benefit after the primary policy has paid
83. **Sleep Apnea** – a temporary stop in breathing during sleep
84. **SOAP documentation – (Subjective, Objective, Assessment, Plan)** – method used to report the provider's focus in the patient's medical condition
85. **Software** – computer programs
86. **Staggered booking** – double or triple line booking with the provider moving from room to room

87. **Subscriber** – the person for which the insurance policy is written
88. **Suppuration** -- also called pus; the yellow, fluid within infected gums
89. **Target audience** – group of people for which a message is meant
90. **Team meetings** – the gathering of two or more members of the same team
91. **Termination Letter** – correspondence informing the termination of employment
92. **The Birthday Rule** – method insurance company uses to determine the primary policy
93. **Third party financing** – funding by an uninvolved entity
94. **Trauma** - serious injury to the body
95. **Treatment planning** –determining the appropriate course of action a clinician will take to correct abnormalities or diseased soft tissue or teeth

96. **Valediction (Complimentary closing)** – signing off of a letter; typically with 'Sincerely', 'Regards' or 'Yours Truly'
97. **Verbal communication** – correspondence in oral form
98. **Verification** – identification of a patient's eligibility within an insurance policy
99. **Waiting period** – the amount of time that a patient must wait before using particular parts of an insurance policy
100. **Written communication** – correspondence in written form; letter, memo, email, etc.

Have you seen our other books?

OMG! Pearls Vol 1

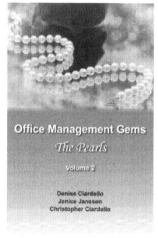
OMG! Pearls Vol 2

All available on Amazon.com

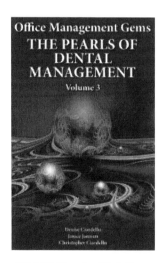
OMG! Pearls Vol. 3

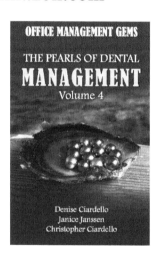
OMG! Pearls Vol. 4

About the Authors

Denise Ciardello
Senior Consultant

Something special happened to Denise on the day she went to get her teeth cleaned; special enough to affect her entire life. There was a practice consultant that approached her at the front desk and offered her a job out of the blue. When Denise replied that she didn't have any dental experience, the consultant said she'd teach her everything she needed to know.

Fast-forward many years, and today Denise is co-founder of Global Team Solutions, a practice management-consulting firm. A professional speaker and published author, her enthusiasm and knowledge about the dental profession has helped many dental teams. She brings experience, insight, and creativity into her management style, along with a sense of humor. In a profession that can cause anxiety in some dental employees, Denise's consulting approach is to partner with doctors and team members to help them realize the dream of creating a thriving, successful practice.

Denise always knew she wanted to be an entrepreneur. She built her business on the foundation of ethics and principles demonstrated by her father, who owned a successful construction company in Houston. Today she is a champion of change, and says the biggest challenge of working with practices is people who think they know it all or are resistant to trying new things. The best parts of Denise's job are those moments when clients "get it," those a-ha moments that can put a practice on the track to serious success.

Along with her talent for business, Denise has gained numerous distinctions in her industry. She is co-author of OMG! Office Management Guide, the "bible" used in training workshops. She is the president of the Academy of Dental Management Consultants and a member of the National Speakers Association, the Hill Country Women in Business, Toastmasters International, and Directory of Dental Speakers. She has been a Certified Dentrix Trainer since 2005, and is a past winner of the Dentrix Trainer of the Year award.

Denise enjoys spending her precious free time with her family. She also loves to shop and work in her yard at home, which is situated in the beautiful Texas hill country. She can be reached at: denise@GTSgurus.com

Denise's Practice Management Tips

DO: Communicate constantly with the doctor to determine their philosophy and vision for the practice. Remember you are there to fulfill their dream of providing excellent patient care.

DON'T: Try to be BFFs with the rest of the team. Nine times out of 10, it will cause problems. Office managers need to lead.

Janice Janssen, RDH, CFE
Senior Consultant

At age 14, Janice got an after-school job working for her dentist. Little did she know how that choice would determine the course of her future. Twenty-something years later, she is the co-founder of Global Team Solutions and an expert in dental practice consulting.

When it comes to working at a dental practice, Janice has seen and done it all. Since her introduction into the field as a teen, she has enjoyed a long career as a dental hygienist and served—and excelled—in many other roles including office management, insurance billing, and collections.

For Janice, the best thing about working in a dental practice is facing the unknown—never knowing what the day is going to hold. She says that can also be the most frustrating thing about it, too. But thanks to her clinical expertise and well-rounded management experience, she has learned to meet every challenge with grace, including the patient who once insisted on clipping her toenails while in the dentist's chair.

Now Janice enjoys consulting because it allows her to share her techniques with the doctors, hygienists, and office staff who are on the front line every day. Her zeal for a proven successful periodontal program makes her a real asset to her clients across the country.

Besides hands-on experience, Janice has gained professional recognition for her hard work and commitment to excellence. She became a Certified Dentrix Trainer in 2004, and was named Dentrix Instructor of the Year in 2013. She is also co-author of OMG! Office Management Guide, the "bible" used in

GTS training workshops. She is also a member of the Academy of Dental Management Consultants (ADMC. And finally, Janice is a Certified Fraud Examiner (CFE), which positions her as an expert in educating dentists to deter fraud and embezzlement in their practice.

In her (rare) spare time, Janice enjoys spending time with family and watching her children play soccer in her hometown of St. Louis, Missouri. She can be reached at: Janice@GTSgurus.com

Janice's Practice Management Tips

DO: Take your time to do things right the first time. (It will take you longer to correct it later.)
DON'T: Sweat the small stuff!

Christopher Ciardello
Consultant

As a kid, Chris Ciardello wanted to travel the world as a famous singer. The gradual realization that he was tone deaf, however, helped guide Chris to his true calling in the dental industry. His grandfather was a dentist and mom Denise had made a successful career out of dental consulting—so Chris eventually took up the "family business." And soon realized he really loved it.

Chris has held key positions in the industry, including practice manager of Dominion Dental Spa. He obtained his Registered Dental Associates certification there since he regularly assisted the doctor in addition to answering phones, greeting patients, and everything in between. At Dominion, Chris learned firsthand how critical dental health can be. Once an unscheduled patient walked in near closing with a painful abscess. After an emergency extraction, the doctor told Chris that the infection was so serious that it could have moved into the bloodstream at any time to affect the heart or brain. The timely extraction may have saved his life.

A natural people person, Chris loved building relationships with patients and staff at the practices where he worked. His upbeat attitude and caring personality have always been a real-life manifestation of the mantra that gets him through tough times: I am positively expecting great results, no matter what I see in front of me. The Universe is rearranging itself for my best interest right now.

Chris's rapport with people and his years in the trenches of practice management have helped him excel in all aspects of practice management

consulting. He became a Certified Dentrix Trainer in 2011, and continues to receive exceptionally high reviews from the offices he serves. And in 2012, he joined Global Team Solutions, where he continues to work today.

Chris holds a bachelor's degree in marketing from the University of Texas, San Antonio. In his spare time, he enjoys yoga and lifting weights, hanging out with friends, and spending time with his dog, Bailey. He can be reached at: chris@GTSgurus.com

Chris's Practice Management Tips

DO: Learn as much as you can about the practice's dental software. Too many offices don't use half the features their software offers, and are missing out on so many ways to save time and money.

DON'T: Jump to conclusions about people. You never know what is going on in their personal life, so if there is a problem they should be treated with empathy and concern.

Global Team Solutions

GTSgurus.com

info@GTSgurus.com